THE
GUIDEBOOK

THE GUIDEBOOK

To the True Secret of the Heart

HIS HOLINESS

M. R. BAWA MUHAIYADDEEN

Volume 1

Library of Congress Catalog Card Number: 75-44557
International Standard Book Number:

First Printing: May, 1976

Printed in the United States of America

Bawa Muhaiyaddeen Fellowship
5820 Overbrook Avenue
Philadelphia, Pa. 19131

Once this form is destroyed and we go beyond, we have to give up the outside form. We have to go beyond the form! Then we meet that Power. If we understand this, we can reach God. Everyone can do this, it is found within everyone. You do not have to go outside in search of this.

My children, who are the gems of my eyes, this is very easy.

BAWA MUHAIYADDEEN

Contents

ACKNOWLEDGMENTS

The discourses presented here were originally given by His Holiness M. R. Bawa Muhaiyaddeen in Tamil, an ancient Dravidian language spoken in southeastern India and Ceylon. They were translated into English by Professor Ajwad Macan-Markar and Dr. M. Z. Markar, both of whom are devoted and close disciples of Bawa.

The work of producing this Guidebook Series was inspired, initiated, and supervised by Bawa himself. Many, many 'children' of the Bawa Muhaiyaddeen Fellowship have contributed their time, energy, and financial support to bring the Wisdom of Bawa's teachings into printed form through these books.

Volume One of this Series, *The Guidebook to the True Secret of the Heart,* is the first major work to be produced completely—from initial translating, recording, transcribing, editing, typing, and proofreading; to book design, typesetting, photographic work, layout, and paste-up; and on through process camera, printing, folding, collating, and even hand binding—by the Fellowship children themselves. Their generosity and hours of ceaseless work are a continuing example of their determination to make known the Truth of God to all who seek it, through the teachings of His Holiness Bawa Muhaiyaddeen.

The forthcoming volumes in this series include discourses by Bawa on: The Wonders of Man's Body, Researching the Mind, The Science of Wisdom, Surrender to God, The Forces of Illusion, The Power of God, and True Peace.

Preface

May all of us find total release from the bondage of selfishness, pride, jealousy, and the dreams of the world, and may we live as one with all who comprise God's One Family. May we see clearly the One Life which exists in Resplendence beyond the veils of multiple forms. *Ameen*.

May all beings who read and re-read this profound and delicate work come to see the meanings within their own hearts and relish the Treasury of Meanings to which we are entitled by Our Creator. May we see how we are united with God. May we become reflections of His Presence and spread His Grace. *Ameen*.

This is a guidebook for those who are called to a moving-toward receptivity of God's Beneficence. It is not so much a descriptive analysis as it is a map to directly receive and become Peace itself. Within that Peace the True Secret of the Heart is revealed.

As each experience and each object within creation is an example of God's Invisible Truth, the living Master, his eternal presence, and his teachings are examples which lead to unity with God. The Master's being in the world exists as an example of God's Being within.

We are set out in a unique kind of striving to achieve Original Unity—the most natural and beautiful harmony—of the limited one within the Unlimited One. All pursuits from the heart are really strivings to find that Harmony.

But we *conceive* of that Unlimited One before actually finding it. By doing this, we fix that One God as an *image* which is, in turn worshipped or continually *in*-tended into our consciousness. This repeated *in*-tending eventually takes a form, a thought form for the intellect or a manifest form for the senses; and that form becomes our god. Because that god came from our conceptions, it is defined by the qualities we possess within our own intentions. That god, formed of our mind and our desires, is made in our own image, the form of ourselves, and remains an abstraction. It is not the God of Life, the Sustainer of the Soul. It is a god of ideas and thoughts. It is a god without fulfillment, taste, absolute certitude, completeness, or permanence. It changes as we change. It does not bestow the explanation of the secrets of existence upon us; it does not give Peace.

Without that Peace we turn toward artistic creativity, psychic and occult powers, magics, political manipulations, technical meditations, and science. We may even doubt that there is meaning in the word *Truth* (fearing that words of certitude might suggest fanaticism). We require instructors with 'recognized' credentials. None of these things are wrong in themselves. They just *are not God*, and thus not the straight path to Peace.

Bawa is credentialed by Boundless Compassion, Clarity, and Love for all lives as his own. This is the dearest credential. He doesn't come to exalt anything other than God. This exaltation surpasses the beauty which the senses can perceive, the intricacies of social systems, the complexities of spiritual technologies, and the scientific criteria of prediction and control. It touches the heart and makes it fragrant with love. The tasting is the testing.

Through the subtle powers of induction and deduction science and intellect can give descriptive accounts for phenomena which have appearance and disappearance. Yet, no matter how subtle science or intelligence may be, they cannot approach the way in which the human being is connected to the Creator. For science, images and symbols are necessary. But God has no image, no figure or symbol; and that part of the human being—the human quality of compassion intermingled with the human dimensions of non-symbolic consciousness—also has no likeness. It must be seen directly, without duality: the seer seeing himself. To investigate this, tools more subtle than imagination can conjure are necessary. The acquisition of these tools has prerequisites. One of these is Peace.

There is no greater science than the investigation of the human being and God. It is the primal root of all meaning. It is the beginning and the end of all human endeavors. But where are we to start. The senses give no indication of God's Presence. We are forced to a going-into our roots, a releasing of our conceptions of how It is, and a rejoining with our own essence. But how is this going-in, this releasing, this mystical re-union to occur.

As in any other pursuit, it is best to find one who has mastered its ways and who can clearly delineate where we are now, and where we are to go. Such a one is very rare. In the past they have come as sages and prophets. They have worn different robes but have always spoken of the Unity of God, the Kingdom of Heaven within, and the Light without shadow.

Bawa comes as the humblest of the humble. He is like an ant. He comes as a student, showing us how to be continually receptive to the unfolding of God's hidden treasures. He is the student who teaches *how to learn*.

The Guide who gives those instructions is unlike the guides who instruct about and within limitation. His speech is silent and eternal. His classroom is the Point of Love within every heart, the Divine One Heart which is connected to all hearts. Neither coming to us nor going from us, He waits with absolute patience for our love to be great enough to accept His Wisdom. To the mind, however, His Words and His Meanings may appear uncanny.

The language of a country to which we have never been may sound strange when we first hear it. The Language which originates in the Country of Human Divinity—a place where meanings transcend the limits of the Tamil of Sri Lanka and the English of the West—might be strange to anyone who has never been to that Country. But the more we study *that* Language, that Metaphor for the Things which are There, the more familar it becomes. And if we should go to *that* Country, we might even begin to think in that Language.

If we say 'table', the *word* is not a table—but with our senses we can have a concurrence of opinion as to what a table is. Within the senses there are reference points for the word. If we say 'Grace', however, there are no sensory reference points (unless we have met such a one as Bawa). The existent to which 'Grace' refers can only be concurred upon through reflection within the Heart, for That is where Grace lives.

This book is a series of Graces given as discourses through His Holiness M.R. Bawa Muhaiyaddeen to lovers of Truth, in Philadelphia during the autumn of 1975. They were expressed in Tamil, an ancient poetic language of South Asia, and arduously translated into English, which is a far less lyrical language. Translating the Unbounded Expressions through two languages is a task that could only be done with extreme diligence and devotion to Truth. It must be read with only that devotion to Truth.

It cannot be understood through comparison with any philosophical system. It is not to be approached reductively. It must be taken on its own terms. Go onto the Path with diligence and devotion, and the proofs will reveal themselves to your self through the Truth within your self.

In order to apprehend the always present simplicity of Truth, we must dig deeper than our normal mental and conceptual delineations would have us. For example, when 'man' is used it should be understood that it does not refer to sexual gender, but to that dimension within life-forms that is distinguished from beast. It refers to the ability to analyze right/wrong, permanent/transient, Truth/falsehood, good/ evil, and to the apprehension of ''who am I.'' The book starts within that level of meaning. The Kingdom of Truth begins at that level.

The meanings of this book are found through our own efforts, through a going in to the Heart and in the Remembrance of God's Grace. It is not a book about what we see. It is a book to understand *who* is seeing. The normal process of absorption in the distracting senses, the configurations of thought, and the willing forgetfulness of God's Presence must be suspended in order to grasp this work. It is a formidable task, but what of value is not formidable?

These are transmissions of an exalted teaching—the Complete Teaching—which in essence is conveyed in the Silence within the deepest recesses of the Heart and Self, and which in manifestation is conveyed largely through spontaneous oral emanation. The Silence is within Re-membering That which was hidden: the Guide is That which reveals and unveils the hiddenness. These Teachings are saturated with the Power of the Master's Transmission. It is a Living Power, and we must animate it through our own inner movements. We must allow Its Power and Guidance to live within our own hearts through our own inner and personal surrender to It.

The heart that holds our emotions and which we even refer to as having form is only an example of the inner formless Heart, or *Qalb*, which holds God's Qualities. It is with this formless, selfless, inner Heart which connects with all hearts, that this subtle book can be understood. Within that inner Heart, *Qalb*, there is the connection with the Master. The connection with the Master is realized when consciousness mixes with compassion and love. Within the resonance of that mixing the history of Bawa Muhaiyaddeen may be properly understood.

Regular Remembrance of God with every breath, every look, every thought, and every speech will fill the Heart with God's Love making a receptacle wherein the Meanings of Peace can Live, and wherein the Secret of the Complete and Pure Heart can be Opened and Revealed. Just as ink needs a page in order to appear as words, so Truth needs the Heart of God's Qualities to appear as Wisdom.

May Love and Perfect Peace flow through us and illumine us in Wisdom so that we have no illusion of separation from the One Guide and Master—God. *Ameen.*

AHAMED MUHAIYADDEEN

Editors' Note

For the world the role of His Holiness M. R. Bawa Muhaiyaddeen is to explain the meanings within all things, to give the explanation of the world and the explanation of human life in the world. For the Soul Bawa's explanation is the Explanation of Wisdom, the Explanation of God, the Explanation which resonates within the Soul itself. In everything that he says, in every meaning that he gives, Bawa clearly distinguishes and defines: what is the world, what is God.

It is the editors' humble intention to present Bawa's words in a visual form which parallels, as faithfully as possible, the clarity of his direct discourse.

Capital letters are used in words referring to God, Wisdom, and the Soul of Man. Tamil and Arabic words which embody particular meanings are introduced with bracketed definitions and are italicized throughout the text. A glossary containing Bawa's explanations for many of the italicized words is also provided.

The spellings of most italicized words are direct transliterations from either the Tamil or Arabic alphabet. Tamil spellings tend to vary slightly from the perhaps more familiar Sanskrit equivalents. The diacritical marks used with Arabic words are chiefly for the benefit of those familiar with Arabic pronunciation, and need not cause confusion to the average reader. A pronunciation key is provided on the reverse side of this page.

May our intention to achieve clarity be fulfilled. May all who read these words of His Holiness Bawa Muhaiyaddeen achieve True Clarity. *Ameen.*

Pronunciation Key

for Arabic and Tamil

Vowel sounds are pronounced as in continental European languages, but with both a short and a prolonged version of each sound. The long mark (ā) indicates that a sound is to be lengthened in time value (not changed altogether as in English). In some words the vowel is actually doubled to produce the long sound.

Consonant sounds are generally the same as in English, with the few exceptions noted below.

a	as in	*a*bove
ā	as in	*fa*ther
e	as in	p*e*tite
ē	as in	pr*ey*
i	as in	p*i*ano
ī	as in	mach*i*ne
o	as in	dep*o*t
ō	as in	*o*ver
u	as in	p*u*t
ū	as in	fr*u*it
ai	as *ie* in	d*ie*
ei	as *ay* in	d*ay*

dh, *dth*, *th* all have a very soft *th* sound.

j in Tamil words is pronounced as *j* in *jar*.

j in Arabic words has a soft *g* sound as in *mirage*.

q in Arabic words is pronounced as a *k* sound; *qu* is pronounced as *ku* (not *kw* as in English).

s sometimes has a slight *sh* sound.

w usually has a very soft *v* sound.

Introduction

To all of the precious children who have Love, Trust, Compassion, and Affection for God. May God's Love come to all of these trusting children.

God is that One Power which is the Unfathomable Treasure, the Incomparable Love. With that Love the tens and tens of millions of creations and their secrets have been created. He has created uncountable numbers of distinctive aspects in His creation: distinctive colors, hues, qualities, languages, faces, and the various aspects of their bodies. He has formed these distinctions from atomic things and from atomless things; from things that move and from things that do not move; from trees, leaves, buds, flowers, fruits, unripe fruits, and ripe fruits; from trees, bushes, colors, hues, qualities, and tastes. He has formed them as many meanings, as many explanations, as many tastes, and as many lights, for many reasons among all things.

God has created the light in gems and encased it within stone. He has created the atomic energies within the earth, fire, water, air, and space; the lights in space, the sun, moon, and stars; the thunder, lightning, and clouds; their sounds, the explanations of the sounds within them, the distinctions and the energies within them, and the explanations of the energies. He has created their languages, their sounds, their explanations, and their qualities. Like this, God has created uncountable creations: birds, little birds, reptiles, things that live in water, things that live in space, and things that live in the earth. He has given them so many languages, sounds, explanations, and colors. All of these languages are in God's creation. They exist in each thing.

The created energies dawned from within God's Power. The colors and hues separated from these energies. There are so many languages that exist within these energies. There are visions, there are faces, there are the sounds of creations with faces and without faces.

All creations are composed of atomic cells. All of these cells exist as forms, as shapes, and as many kinds of creations. They can exist as trees, they can exist as flowers, they can exist as animals, they can exist as men. Like this, there are many effects produced from these cells, all of which are energies and forces revealed from God's Power.

In all of His creations, God has created these languages, sounds, explanations, smells, and fragrances so that what is revealed can be identified. It is through their smells, their fragrances, their qualities, and their sounds that the creations can be given names. It is through the perception of their smells and their qualities that they can be identified. They can all be seen on the outside. One who perceives these things, one to whom this explanation comes, one who can distinguish this point and see it is called a Man. That is what is called Man.

The outer form of man is like the form of animals; both forms are made of earth, fire, water, air, and space. That is man's form, his body. He has a body and the animal has a body. On the inside there is another Form for what is known as Man. That Form is God's Form. That Form consists of God's Qualities, God's Justice, God's Compassion, and the Form of the Duty which He performs. That is the Form of God's Qualities. The Trustee which can understand this is Wisdom. The Trustee of that Kingdom is Wisdom. That is the Money of that Kingdom, the Wealth of that Kingdom. That is the Trustee of God. Wisdom is the Money of that Kingdom and that Form is the Trustee—God. That Form is His Justice. That Wisdom is the Money. It is inside.

The Money that is Wisdom can be used everywhere. It can be put into any bank. It can be put into the Bank of the Trustee of God. That Bank of the Trustee of God is God's Love, Compassion, Peacefulness, and Justice; these are the Trustee of God. That is the Peacefulness and the Bank, the All Bank. It is a Bank belonging to all districts, the Unity Bank. It is a Bank for all the creations that God has created. Everything can be put into it. The Trustee can be put within it. Patience, Compassion, Tolerance, Peacefulness, Justice, Integrity, Tranquility, Quietness, and Duty—God's Duty— all these Qualities can be deposited into it and withdrawn from it. That is the Bank. That is the Trustee's Bank. All of those Forms made by Wisdom can be placed within it. It can be deposited into and withdrawn from. God's Kingdom is inside. That is the Bank of God's Kingdom. One who knows this Wisdom, this Bank, this Trustee—one who knows this Explanation—is Man.

There is wrong and there is Right. Understanding the Treasures of Heaven and the treasures of hell, discarding the treasures of hell and accepting the Treasures of Heaven, and depositing the Treasures of Heaven into that Bank is the Bank of the Kingdom of God. The Trustee cannot accept the treasures of hell. He must accept the Treasures of Heaven. He must see what is wrong and what is Right, distinguish and separate them, take God's Treasures and give them to Him, and discard and throw away all other treasures. One who understands this is called a Man. One who knows this is a Man. One who has that Form is a Man. One who has that Trustee is a Man. The Trustee of that Wisdom is the Money, the undiminishing Wealth to his life. That is the Treasure of Peace, that is Peace. That Bank can be withdrawn from and deposited into. That is Man's Bank, the Peace Bank, the Trustee Bank.

The outside bank is earth, fire, water, air, and ether. The body bank, the form bank is earth, fire, water, air, ether, mind, and desire. These seven have joined together to form this cooperative bank. Mind and desire withdraw from and deposit into this bank. The managers of this bank are illusion, satan, desire, the monkey mind, and torpor or darkness. These five conduct the cooperative bank, they are the managers. These are the seven and the five.

This cooperative bank can change at any time. These seven and five can separate, withdraw their shares, and change at any time. They can steal. One can separate from another, one can eat another, one can destroy another, one can steal from another. That is what they can do. This bank of the body can change at any time, it can be destroyed, it can change. It is not the Natural Bank, it is a cooperative bank. Many, many things can be kept within it.

It is a supermarket. Many, many tens and tens of millions of beings speaking tens and tens of millions of languages will come to the supermarket to buy things.

Languages, scriptures, religions—everything will come to buy at the supermarket. Each will bring his own language, each will bring his own speech, recitation, and form. Lions, tigers, bears, birds, snakes, scorpions, satans, demons, *jinns*, fairies, ants, fire, fruits, ripe fruits, trees, fish—all those things will come, and each will come to speak with its own language. This is the supermarket. All languages will be there, all of these languages will be there.

Man has an inside Form and an outside form. He has two forms. The inside Form is the Trustee of God. God's Qualities exist as His Form. The Trustee for that Kingdom, the Trustee for that Form, is Wisdom. That is the Money, that is the Wealth of that Kingdom. The outside form is the form of the five elements.

At the time of the creation of the outside form, at the dawning of that form's energy, it speaks all languages. When that form is taken, when it is born, when it comes out, when it takes form and shape with the five elements, when it is coming out after the months of pregnancy, when the outside form is being brought out—that form which comes out speaks all languages. It speaks the language of little birds, the language of atoms, the language of ants, the language of fish, the language of snakes, the language of animals, the language of bulls, the language of peacocks, the language of water, the language of air, the language of fire, the language of lights, the language of musical melodies—all languages. It speaks the language of *om* and the language of *aum*, the language of *ing* and *hum*, the language of *him*, the language of *hoo*, the language of *om*, the language of *aum*, the language of *ee*, the language of *ayeyee*, the language of *inga*, and uncountable, limitless languages—all languages.

It performs all actions and it speaks all languages. It destroys many things, it catches and bites many things. It performs everything except for these three: sexual love; the arrogance of the world (what is *mine*, *my* house, *my* possessions); and what is known as the 'I'. In its movements that infant performs the 64 arts and sciences and the 64 sexual arts—like the sex of birds, the sex of snakes, and their types of love. Grasping its heart the infant performs all of these things.

It even does what the earth does. It speaks all languages. It behaves like snakes, beasts, bulls, and everything. It seems like *māya* [illusion]. It seems like a bull, it seems like a tiger. It shrieks like a satan. All of these sections and languages are displayed within the infant. It makes love to so many of those beasts, it makes love to all of those demons, it makes love to all desires, it makes love to torpor, it makes love to the beasts, it makes love to the snakes, scorpions, trees, bushes, and many other things. It makes love to all of those forms. All of those qualities have form within the infant. They come inside his form. These languages are the languages learned before, these are the ways learned before, this is the love learned before. There are forms like this which exist within the infant.

There are two forms which exist within man. There is the outside form and there is the inside Form. The Treasury is what explains the outside form and the inside Form. The inside Form is God's Trustee, the outside form is hell's trustee. Mind and desire are the trustees for hell. Man's outside form belongs to hell.

None of the aspects of the mind have any peace, or tranquility. There are so many languages within the mind. So many languages, the previous creations, and sexual love are all within it, so there is no peace for it. That mind is the monkey, illusion, satan, and the baby. That is why it will never have peace, not even for one day. It cannot be made peaceful. That is the outside form.

What can make the two sections peaceful is Peace—the Trustee. The inside Trustee is Wisdom. Separating the two sections, giving the mind's trust to the mind, and God's Trust to God is Peace—Tranquility. One who has the Wisdom to understand this, one who has the Wisdom to understand what is Right and what is wrong is Man. That is the Son of God—Man. The state of this mind is like the cooperative store. The other state is that of God's Kingdom, the state of the Trustee. One is the supermarket, the cooperative store. That is hell. Hell is the state of the cooperative, or the supermarket. The other is the state of God's Trustee, the state of His Kingdom.

God has created Divine Analytic Wisdom so that this can be understood. For other beings there may be one state of consciousness, two, three, four, or five states of consciousness. These five states of consciousness are the consciousness of the five elements. Satan's consciousness is the consciousness of the darkness of ignorance; the consciousness of illusion is torpor. These two, satan and illusion, are complete darkness, ignorance, and torpor. These two aspects will hide the five levels of consciousness. The darkness of ignorance and the torpor of illusion will hide the five levels of consciousness. They will hide them. That is then the seven hells. As soon as the concealment takes place, that is hell. That is the supermarket, the cooperative store.

For the inside Form of Man, however, there is the sixth state of consciousness, Divine Analytic Wisdom. That is the Wisdom which distinguishes, separates, and sees. That sixth state of consciousness is the Wisdom which distinguishes, separates, and sees.

Among beings with five states of consciousness there are those who speak. They might be like men or they might be like animals. They might be like snakes, they might be like birds, they might be like bulls, they might be like donkeys, they might be like horses, they might be like dogs, they might be like cats, they might be like many things. They might have men's faces, or they might have animals' faces. They might be like monkeys or they might be like men; both of these can have five states of consciousness. They defecate where they eat and lie down where they defecate; they drink water at one end and urinate at the other; they experience pleasure in one place and then lick that place; they do something foul or have sex, and then they lick themselves. These are animals without Divine Analytic Wisdom. They defecate where they eat and lie down where they defecate. They experience the pleasure of sex in a certain place and then lick that place. Those who do not have Divine Analytic Wisdom might look like animals or like men. They may speak many languages, they may have many sounds, they may have many kinds of music, they have many beauties, they may have many colors.

One who has Wisdom and who distinguishes, one who looks at what is Right and what is wrong and understands with Wisdom, one who understands what is Right and what is wrong, one who understands that this is Right and that is wrong—that one is the Son, Man, the Trustee. He is the Trustee of God. His Wealth is the Ocean of Divine Knowledge. It is Wisdom. The Wisdom of Grace, the Wisdom of Truth, the Wisdom of Light, the Wisdom of God—that is God's Trustee. With that Wisdom everything can be distinguished and seen.

Distinguishing and seeing what is Tranquility and what is not Tranquility; what is Calmness and what is not Calmness; what is Indestructible and what is not Indestructible—understanding that, discarding all of the destructible things, and giving the Indestructible Treasure to the Trustee of God is the work of the Trustee. This is the Treasure of the Trustee of God. Who is the Trustee for this Treasure? God. For this Wealth God alone is the Trustee.

Who is the trustee for the other things, for the cooperative store? Satan, illusion, mind, and desire—they are the trustees for those things. They are the trustees which can be destroyed and consumed. They catch and eat each other. The one who knows the Explanation and who understands the Justice of the Justice Court is Man. The others are just languages and sounds. To attain Peace without this Explanation and without this Understanding is difficult. No matter how many languages one learns, no matter how many languages are known, if one comes shouting and yelling to attain Peace, it is very difficult.

If one uses sounds that came forth at the birth of the form of the five elements—if one uses *am*, *am*, *am*, *eem*, *heem*, *reeng*, *oong*, *mmng*, *ahng*, *eeng*, *aye*, *yee*, *ooh*, *ah*, *oo*, *oo*, *ahng*, *reeng*—these are all sounds which came before. They are all sounds that he spoke at the time of birth. If he speaks those same sounds now, he cannot attain Peace with them. *Aagh! Aagh! Aagh!* These are sounds that he would make if he were a dog. This *meow*, *meow*, *meow* is the sound of a cat. If one were a parrot, he would make the *kee*, *kee*, *kee*, *kee*, *kee* sound. If he were a bird he would say *ooo*, *ooo*, *ooo*, *ooo*, *ooo*—or *ah*, *ah*, *ah*, *ah*—like an owl. *Am-am-am-am* is the sound a puppy makes. A bull says *amoo*, *amoo*, *amoo*, *amoo*. A goat says *maah*, *maah*, *maah*. *Ungum*, *ungum*, *ungum*, *ungum* is the sound a calf makes.

Those are sounds. They are sounds that some people make. But all of those sounds that they make are dog sounds, cat sounds, rat sounds, and bird sounds. If one uses those sounds as *mantras* [chants, formulas, or incantations], he can never achieve peace. Peace will never come to one in that state.

The *karma* incurred at the time of birth is causing so much trouble now. Sometimes one can be like a bull. If he makes the bull's sound, he is a bull. Sometimes one can be like a snake, sometimes like a lion. Sometimes one can be like a demon or like a ghoul. Sometimes one can be like a beast, a lion, or a tiger. Sometimes one can be like a bird, sometimes like a vulture. Sometimes one can be like a hyena, sometimes like a fox, sometimes like a dog, sometimes like a cat, sometimes like a rat, sometimes like a crow, sometimes like a chicken, sometimes like a stork standing on one leg meditating, sometimes like a pig, sometimes like a donkey, sometimes like a horse carrying things. Sometimes he is a monkey performing tricks he has seen before. There are so many tricks within him. All of the tricks that were performed before, exist within him now. And all of the sounds he made before, he makes now.

The qualities of those sounds all exist within him. The sounds, the qualities, the forms, and the noises all exist within him. They exist in the earth—in form—in fire, in water, in air, in space, in mind, and in desire. Possessing within himself all of these tens and tens of millions of things, will there be peace for him in doing these *mantras* of the elements? He can never attain peace by saying the *mantras* which he said before. There is no peace in doing that. Hell does not have peace. You must think about this.

Children, gems within my eyes, think about this a little. Know what is wrong· and what is Right. Then the Trustee of God's Peace will understand who is the trustee to which kingdom. There are states of consciousness from one to six. All beings that do not have Divine Analytic Wisdom, all beings that do not have the Wisdom to know what is Right and what is wrong—whether they have the faces of men or the faces of beasts, whether they are monkeys or whether they are dogs, and no matter how many languages they know—for all the time that goes by without the Explanation of Wisdom, and as long as wrong and Right are not known, those beings will have only the qualities that existed before. That is the cooperative store kingdom. That is the supermarket kingdom. The trustees are satan, illusion, mind, and desire. These are the trustees of hell.

One who is a Trustee of Heaven is one who has the Trustee of God—that Wisdom which distinguishes and sees. The Form of the Qualities of God will not harm any life, it will not cause pain to any heart. It will become the Beauty of Compassion. That Trustee will regard others' lives as his own life, he will regard the hunger of others as his own, he will regard the sorrow of others as his own, he will regard the happiness of others as his own, and he will regard the lives of others as his own. He will regard others as he regards himself. The Wisdom which makes him regard others as he regards himself is Divine Analytic Wisdom. That is Man. That is Man's Wisdom. That section has two forms. One Form exists inside. The other form exists outside; the form of the five elements exists outside. Man needs to understand these two forms. This belongs to the earth and that belongs to Heaven.

Of the two, which did he appear from? From where did this form appear? From hell—from earth, fire, water, air, and ether. Semen, desire, mind, thoughts, arrogance, *karma*, and illusion—where did they appear from? From the fluids of the blood, from earth, from fire, from water, from air, and from ether. From the black hole—hell. Man's form belongs to the hell of fire. He came from that and he goes back into it. He first came as form from what was his mother. He goes back into that again for love and he gets buried within it. That is hell. It will consume him. He came from within it, he returned to it, and he will get buried there. That form is hell.

But the Form which came from God is the Light Form. God's Light Form, His Treasury of Grace, His Resplendent Form came from Him and will go back to Him. The form of the elements will go there [to hell], and this Form will go to God. One who understands this is Man. If one has that Wisdom, he is called Man. If that Wisdom is not there, one cannot be called a Man. Having that Wisdom is the State of Peace. One who understands this is in the State of Peace. That is Divine Knowledge, Wisdom.

It is only after Wisdom has come, after one has realized and understood it, that he has Peace. That is the Trustee of God. The Trustee of God, that Wisdom, is God's Wealth. That is the Money, that is His Money in all the worlds. That is the Gem, that is His Life. It is that Life which is Wealth for him. One who realizes this State is Man. That is Peace. Then the Heart becomes a Flower Garden and that Fragrance will come there.

Gems within my eyes, you need to think. We can perceive the taste and fragrance in all things—in leaves, in everything. Please think about it and look at it. The rose fragrance exists in the rose flower. A jasmine tree has a jasmine fragrance. A lemon has a distinct fragrance. An orange has a distinct fragrance. A mango has a distinct smell. A banana has a distinct smell. A jack fruit has a distinct fragrance. Each leaf has a distinct scent. Mint has a scent. Like this, when we perceive these flowers and fragrances on the outside, we can tell what each is by its fragrance. This is this, this, or this flower—then we can give it a name. Each thing has a distinct taste, and we can tell about it from its taste. Taste exists like that in everything—in goats, in cattle, in everything. Each thing has a smell, and from the smell of its perspiration we can perceive if it is a goat or a cow. We can distinguish all tastes in this way, and we can perceive smells and distinguish them. But these are all things that we can perceive on the outisde. They exist as things which can be understood. Everything has an identification like that, a point like that.

What identification is there for man? What smell does he have? How can that smell be perceived? Everything else—each flower and each animal has a smell or a scent. But what does man have? He has only stench. This must be thought about and looked at a little.

Man has a stench, a very sweaty smell. He has all sorts of things collected inside of him, and when he tries to use the scents of flowers and trees on the outside, that becomes smell upon smell. On the outside, man's body has a very bad odor. Even though he uses the essences of flowers and buds, he uses them only on the outside. He uses them on the outside form to try to hide stench. He uses them to cover over his smell. He uses one smell to cover over another. That becomes smell upon smell!

Everything displays an identifying scent. Man too has to have such an identifying fragrance, does he not? He must have a fragrance. Man's Fragrance is that of the Trustee of God. Everything else displays its fragrance on the outside, but Man's Fragrance is on the inside. That is the *Qalb*, the Heart. The Form built with Wisdom is the *Qalb*. This is the Flower Garden.

The other is the mind, the chest. What is within it are the five elements—one fistful of earth. That is what the stench is. That stench can be perceived on the outside. Man's stench, the stench of the body, is perceived on the outside. Everything else has a fragrance or a scent, but man's body has a stench. That stench is the 'fragrance' in his body. What is in his mind is fragrant to him, that is the stench. The mind is stench, the body is stench. A flower has fragrance, but man's food and nourishment and all that he eats smell bad. This is the stench. This body is stench. No matter what he tries to use on it, he cannot conceal that stench. This form which he has taken is not Man. Man is Original. What came from hell is stench, what rolled around is stench, the egg he came from is stench, the embryo is stench, what came from that is stench, his form is stench. That stench is the fragrance of his form. The stench comes from his body like fragrance comes from a flower. This must be thought about a little.

What Man is, is not this form. One thing is the form that came from hell, the other is the Form that came from the Trustee of God. The Fragrance of the Trustee must come forth. That Form is called the *Qalb*, the Flower Garden. That is the Flower Garden, the Lotus of the Heart, the Rose Flower. The Fragrance of that Garden is very sweet. That is what can be perceived by Wisdom. That Flower Garden can be perceived by God's Qualities. It is inside. That is Man. That is Man's Fragrance. The Fragrance of that Form is known to God, it is the Fragrance which God imbibes. It is the Son of God. It is that Fragrance which He imbibes.

When that Flower blooms, God will take it. He will come with His Sound to take the Natural Honey which is there. The Honey, the Fragrance, its Beauty—its great, great Beauty will be there. When that Flower of the Heart blooms, God will come and He will take that Trustee, that Fragrance, into His Kingdom. He will give His Kingdom to that Form, to the Son. That State is *Shānti* [Peace], that is Tranquility, that is Peace. This is the Trustee for Man.

The other is the trustee for the mind and for the stench

of the mind. No matter how many forms one takes, no matter how many flowers, colors, hues, perfumes, or fragrant scents he uses on himself, there will be no peace. No matter how many *mantras* or magics or *aah-eee-oos* he uses, there will be no peace. Peace will not come, True Peace will never come to that. That is stench, that is hell. Peace will never come to it.

Gems of my eye, children of Wisdom, if you want the State of Peace, you must understand what True Peace is for Man. If the mind of man is to attain Peace—if you want this—please read this Peace book, read this Peace book again and again. This is a book of my experiences, this Peace book. The State of God's Peace is True Peace for the mind. Please analyze this book a little. You must distinguish and see the state before your birth, the state of the embryo having been formed, the state of your life now—how you were formed, where you came from, the state of your body now, your outside life, and the inside Life of Wisdom—the Life of the Soul. To understand and to reach Peace, to live Peacefully, you must understand this Point.

This is my experience. Please do not throw it away. Read this book with Peacefulness again and again and again. Please take up this book and look at it whenever the mind begins to worry or be disturbed. Look at it just a little. Pick it up and look at it whenever the mind becomes disturbed. When sadness comes, take this book and look at it. When the mind brings forth sorrow, take this book and look at it a little. This is the book of the True State of Peace for the mind of man. That State is God's Explanation of Grace, the Radiance of Man's Wisdom. It is Radiance to Wisdom. This is the State of True Peace for the mind. This is the Trustee. This is the Trustee for Peace of mind, for Peace to the heart. The Wealth is Wisdom. The Trustee for Peace of mind, for Peace to the heart, is Wisdom.

Please think about this a little. *Ameen.*

May your intentions of Peace and Peacefulness be fulfilled. *Ameen.*

Peace

My children, who are the jewels of my eyes, my dearest children in America, on the continent of Europe, and all the children of this world, you must realize that there is One God. His Secret is within you, and your secret is within Him. His Peace is within you, and your peace is within Him. Your food is within Him. That food of love which you give to Him is within Him. Like this, there are many beautiful qualities and actions that you have to realize. God has created Man as the most beautiful form. Within Man, God has placed His Grace and His $Z\bar{a}t$ [Essence]. Man must keep God's Wisdom, His Qualities, and His Strength within himself. God has placed within Man the Most Gracious Qualities and the Most Gracious Actions. He has placed that Truthful and Complete Treasure there. You must return to Him His Qualities, His Love, and His Compassion. This is the secret of Man. In the life of Man, this is a very subtle secret. It is not like any other creations that God has created. It is not like any other actions which God has created. It is not like any other of the creations of God.

Out of the six types of lives, the Soul of Man is that Ray which came from God. This is a Light to the world. The Human Soul is a Light to the body. It is a Ray which came from God. God is All-Pervasive; He is Plenitude.

My children, you must therefore reflect on this. God says: ''I created Man as the most exalted Form of My Wealth. In order that he may see, perceive, and feel Me, I have given him seven lights. In order that he may realize Me, I have given him feeling, awareness, intellect, judgment, Wisdom, Divine Analytic Wisdom, and Divine Luminous Wisdom (which is the *Noor*, the Plenitude of the Light). I have given him these seven levels of Wisdom, and if he uses them he will see Me. He is My secret, and I am his Secret. Man has to understand Me through his seven levels of Wisdom. I will understand Man through his heart. I will understand him through his breath, through his looks, through his speech, through his heart, through his actions, through his conduct, and through his qualities. But Man, using these seven treasures of Wisdom, must see Me. Having understood Me, having understood My Wealth, having understood My Qualities, having understood My Actions, and having understood My Compassion —if he obtains My Beauty—he will see Me and I will see Him.''

This is the Explanation that God gave. This Beautiful State is called Man. This is his Prayer. Understanding the Explanation, the Resonance, the Clarity, the Resplendent Wisdom, the Light of the Soul, and the connection between the Son and the Plenitude of God is Prayer.

There are no *mantras*. This Prayer has no *mantras*.

God says, "We have given this Explanation to Man alone." Through His Limitless Grace and His Limitless Compassion, God preached to Man. The one who obtains this Strength and this Power is Man. This is that Power. The Power of Man is the Power of God. God's Power is that Power which is contained in those seven treasures of Wisdom. But, my children, there are certain things that we have to realize. You must realize these states of Wisdom. Children, who are now in this country and in the rest of the world, it is only through these states that you reach that Peace which is Peace to your Soul. The Love of God, His Grace, and His Wealth—this is *Shānti*, or True Peace of Mind.

My children, who are the gems of my eyes, you have four sections within you: you must understand who you are, you must know who God is, you must also research that Point which makes you grow, and you must understand the cause and the effects of your body. These should be reflected upon and understood through Wisdom. In your form there are four sections or four causes. Including the mind, there are five causes. Earth is the section in which you are born—that is your body. Fire is the aspect of your hunger, your aging, and your illness—that is hell. Earth belongs to the creation of *māya* or illusion; fire is the fire of hell; air, or the vapors, is the air for the four hundred trillion, ten thousand types of lives. There are many kinds of air, which are also called vapors. They can be the vapors of ghosts, the vapors of the soul, the vapors of the angels, the vapors of satan, the vapors of *māya*, the vapors of demons, or the vapors of the senses. Everything you see in creation exists within man. There are vapors and there is Pure Vapor. There are so many vapors.

To create man God took one fistful of earth. He made

3

that fistful of earth into the heart of man. He condensed and placed everything within this heart: the 18,000 universes, *māya*, satan, the seven hells, and the seven oceans—the silver ocean, the black ocean, the blood ocean, the blue ocean, the golden ocean, the ocean of *māya*, and the ocean of desire. There are seven oceans within the heart of man. The 18,000 universes are found within this heart. This is the city of *māya*, it is the city of magic, it is the city of demons. It is a jungle where beasts exist and live. It is a whirlpool. It is a section that lives on air. There are many currents in it; there are many magnetic forces in it. The forces of demons are within it, the forces of *jinns* are within it, the forces of angels are within it, the forces of satan are within it, the forces of *mantras* are within it. Like this, there are four hundred trillion, ten thousand different types of forces which exist within the heart—within this fistful of earth.

Within these forces are the world, satan, torpor, the baby [mind], and the seventy battalions of monkeys. Within these forces are religions, glitters, and birth; arrogance, *karma*, *māya*, and the three sons of *māya*—*Tārahan*, *Singham*, and *Sūran*. There are also the ties of birth and the ties of *karma*. Then there are the six evils: lust, anger, miserliness, attachments, hatred, and envy. The five sins—intoxication, sex, theft, murder, and falsehood—are also within these forces.

These 17 worlds are there in the heart. In Tamil these are called the *purānas* [epics]. They belong to the world of *māya*. ·This is where satan dwells, this is where illusion dwells, this is where darkness dwells. This aspect is the mind. This is what is called the mind, or the heart. All these things exist within this mind or heart.

God also exists in one section of this heart. God lives in one section, and *māya* lives in another section. The heavens

and paradise are there. Hell is there. All these aspects are there.

My children, who are the jewels of my eyes, you have to reflect upon this. The *qalb* [the heart or mind] contains all these things. It is not a thing that just exists. God sent down 124,000 prophets so that you may realize who you are. There are eight purified prophets. There are 25 prophets who are like the presidents of the prophets. Some of these are: Adam, Noah, Jonah, Joseph, Job, Abraham, David Solomon, Ishmael, Moses, Jesus, and Muhammed. There are 25 prophets who have been selected out of the total number of prophets. From among the 25, God has selected eight pure prophets. Through these eight prophets, He has given the Explanation of God. He has divided the prophets into four sections: the forces of earth, the forces of fire, the forces of water, the forces of air, and also the forces of the eyes. (The religion of Islam relates to vision, sounds, smell, and speech.)

The first of these four sections is Hinduism, which is related to birth. Hinduism is Adam, the creations of Adam. The second is the religion of fire worship, which belongs to fire. Fire is also known as the angel of death, *'Izrā'eel*. Then there is water. Michael is the angel of water. *Isrāfīl* is the angel of air. Like that, there are four angels. These four angels comprise this body. We have to think about this.

Mind is the ether. That is what we call illusion or *māya*. There are many stars which exist in space. The moons exist in the ether as well as the sun, clouds, the colors, the different hues, the thunder, the lightning, the rains, the sun, and the heat. These things which exist in the ether are the mind. This mind is what we call ether or space. It is the thing that continuously changes in the same way the sky changes. Because these things like the colors in the ether are seen,

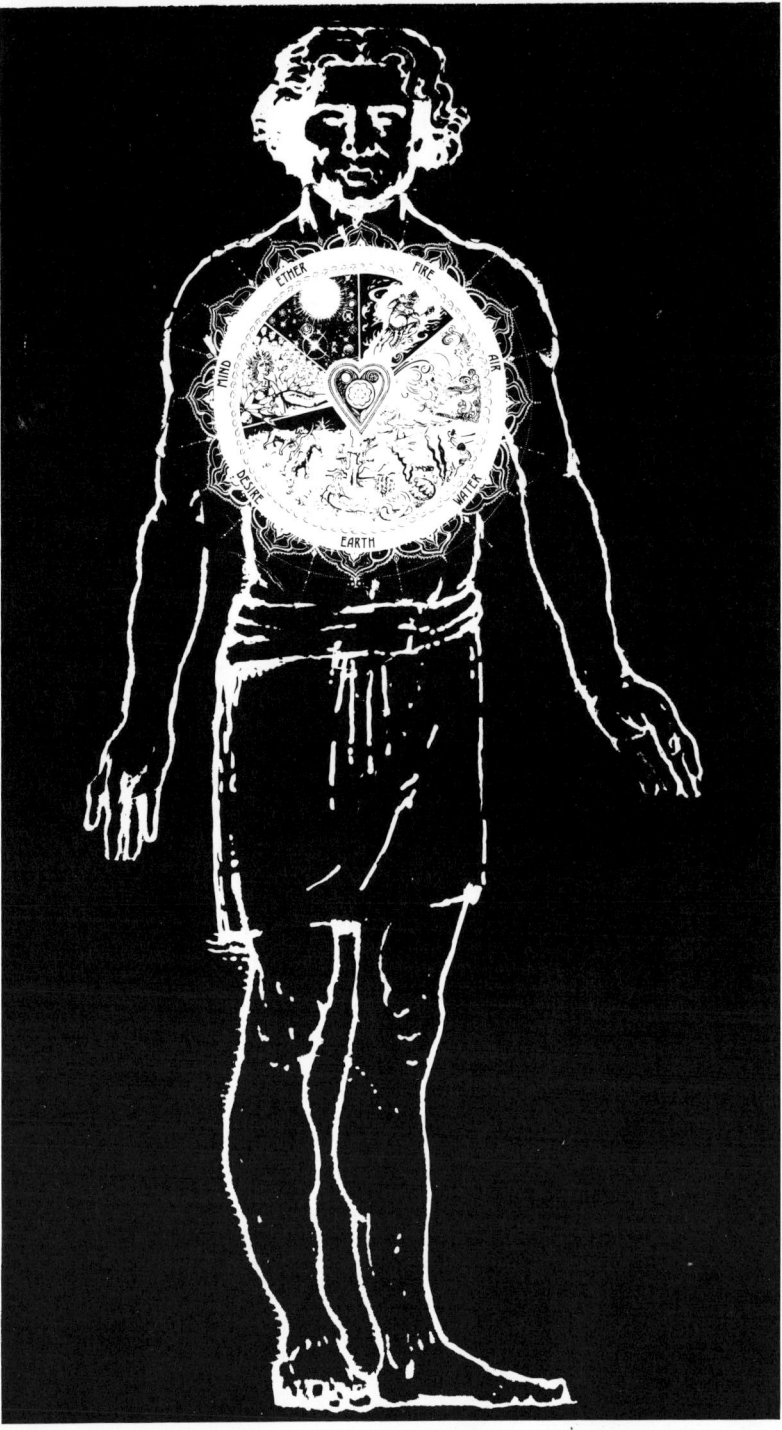

and because these points move like the waves of the mind, they are called the mind.

All the smoke and all the things we see now can be seen in the ocean of *māya*. These stars can be seen in the ocean of *māya*, the moon can be seen in the ocean of *māya*, and the sun can be seen in the ocean of *māya*; all these shadows can be seen in the ocean of *māya*, but they are not really there. What you see is only a reflection. When you look at the ocean of *māya* you see the stars there, and when you look up you see the same stars above you. It is the waves of this world we see in our mind. We think we see *Gnānam* [Wisdom], we think we see Light, we think we see the sun, we think we see the moon and the stars. We see all these in the ocean of *māya* which is the mind. All those things which have appeared are seen in the ocean of our mind—they appear like waves, they come and go like waves, they come and go like the tides, they come and go like the clouds. Like this, we see these things in the mind. All these are seen in the mind.

What we perceive in the mind, however, is not reality—this is what we call the mind or *māya*. The elements look at this and enjoy it, but this is part of *māya*, this is the magic of *māya*. This does not belong to the section of Man or Man's Wisdom. Just as the moon and the stars disappear when the sun appears, the glitters of the mind disappear when the Wisdom of Man appears. These things that glitter in the night are glitters of the mind. As soon as the sun comes up, the moon, the stars, and all the other lights which glitter in the darkness lose their strength, and they lose their force. When the sun appears, the clouds, the waves, and the smoke begin to move away. What you saw in the darkness cannot be seen in the sunlight. In this ocean of *māya*, which is the mind, it is like this. As soon as Wisdom dawns the things you see in your mind will

disappear, just as the moon and the stars disappeared when the sun dawned. When the Light of Wisdom dawns within you all the things you see with your mind will disappear. The lights, the glitters, the stars, and the moons will disappear. The things that are found in the ether disappear.

Then the waves of the elements will try to come. They are like the clouds found in the colors, the races, and the religions. These things will try to hide you. These are the things which keep moving like the clouds in the sky. These are the bloodties and the blood connections. They will try to cover you just as the clouds try to cover the sun. The clouds keep moving. Every second they change.

There are the four seasons, and there are the four periods of time. In the ocean of *maya* the tide moves in eight directions: the tide will come from the east to the west, at another time it might move from west to east, then the tide might move from south to north, at some other time it might move from north to south. Like this, the tide flows in eight directions. In one day you will find the tide moves in eight different directions—that movement of the tide is there. The waves in this ocean of *maya*, which is the mind, move in eight directions. When it moves in one direction, one section is at peace. When it comes in the reverse direction, the other section is at peace. When it comes from the north to the south, the north will be at peace but the south will be in turmoil. Then the reverse occurs. One section will be in turmoil, and the other section will be at peace. When the tide moves on one side there are no waves; when the tide moves in the opposite direction there are no waves on the other side. Like that, the tide will change in these eight directions.

This *karma* of our birth moves in one direction. As soon as a person becomes a victim of sex there is no other

direction for him—his entire concentration is on sex, none of the other things seem to work, only sex is working at that time. There are no other waves that operate then, the rest of that person is in a state of peace. The thing which he is focused on is sex. When that is over, the tide starts moving westward. From the east it moves towards the west. Once this sex act is over, his strength is gone, his nerves are weak, and he is tired and fatigued. Those two minutes or five minutes which he enjoyed while the tide moved in that direction made him tired. There is peace on that side because there are no more waves there.

Then the tide might move in another direction, and suddenly fire might appear. That is the fire of hunger. Hunger appears because this fire starts to burn. At this time he wants to look for food. This is the next step. There is peace in one section, but now hunger is afflicting him. Next, when the tide moves to the north, air comes into play. Then comes aging. What does he need now? The elements have to be fed with air. That is needed when he is aging. When the tide moves from south to north, there is peace in the south. Like this, the mind runs in four directions. While it is running in one direction there is peace in the other directions. That is the mind. The waves run in eight directions. You have to understand this.

Whatever you may understand, you must realize that only the Words of God and the Commandments of God will give you Peace. This is a school for you. We have to understand this school, this university. It is our Father's Book, which He has given us. He has given us a Book which is kept in our treasury. It is like a book of horoscopes. It is something you have to know. It is like a dictionary. You have to have Wisdom to understand the meanings which are given in this dictionary. You have to look with Wisdom for the meanings in this dictionary. All the explanations are given in this dictionary, all of God's creations are found in it, His Whole Treasury is in it. There may be many tens and tens and tens and tens and tens of millions of languages in this dictionary. The language of ants, the language of birds, the language of fish, the language of elephants, the language of horses, the language of rats, the language of cats, the language of fairies, and the language of man are found within this dictionary. There are millions and millions of languages in this dictionary. Since there are many different languages within it, you need human wisdom to refer to it. You have to be one who knows all of those languages. With your knowledge of them and with that wisdom you can look at the dictionary. Then you can understand the meanings and make each being peaceful. It operates this way.

My children, who are the gems of my eyes, you have to reflect on this now. For these reasons God sent down the prophets and His Commandments—so that we may refer to our dictionary and read His Story. That is why we have come to this earth.

My children, who are the gems of my eyes, please reflect on these four sections: first, you have to understand who you are; second, you have to understand who God is; next, you have to understand on whom you are meditating; then you have to understand who attains Peace. These things you have to know. What is your period of time or estimate? Who is man? Who is God? What is life? What is peace? You have to understand all these things. My children, you must understand this with your Wisdom.

Now I am studying the way you are searching for peace in America, Africa, Europe, and Asia. Peace should come through the Commandments of God. You must know what that Peace is which you have to obtain. You are trying to create peace, and you are reciting so many tens of millions of *mantras*. You are reciting many tens of millions of languages and so many tens of millions of *mantras*, but you are not accepting the prophets who came through the Commandment of God. In reality, you do not have the wisdom to study what those Commandments mean. In truth, the Commandment of God is not a business, it is not a *mantra*, and it is not a *tantra* or trick.

God's Command is that thing which flows through Compassionate Love. It flows through God's Actions, God's Qualities, and God's Conduct. It is a thing which is understood through His Treasury which is the *Qalb* [the Heart]. It is the Wisdom which radiates from the Soul, the Light. That Light has 3,000 Attributes or Qualities. Each of these Gracious Qualities is the Quality of God. There are 3,000 heads and 6,000 hands which belong to each of those Divine Qualities. To each of these Compassionate Qualities there are 3,000 heads and 6,000 hands. These 3,000 Divine Attributes, the celestial beings, and the messengers protect you. They give you Peace and prevent dangers from attacking you. They protect Man, the Son of God. God has created 3,000 angels which are like the secrets of the Kingdom of God. If you develop Wisdom and faith in God, if you have accepted the Truth and the Commandments which the prophets brought to you, and if you have accepted the One God, that One *Allāhu*, then you will be protected. You will be given that protection.

You must have His Qualities in order to meditate. You must have His Qualities of Love, you must have His Qualities of Affection, you have to try to form these Qualities. To study and understand this dictionary and the languages in it you need the Wisdom of Grace. You need an *Insān Kāmil*—a perfect Man, a True Guru, a Saint, a great Saint. It is through this great Saint, the *Insān Kāmil*, that you are able to obtain this Wisdom. It is through the station of *Qutbiyat* [the

Wisdom which Explains] that you receive this Wisdom and the Qualities of God.

This is not a business, it is not a *mantra*. It is not a *mantra* for meditation. To imbibe and to reflect upon the Qualities of God is meditation, to love Him is meditation, to trust Him is your meditation, to bring His Actions into action is meditation, to bring God's Conduct into your conduct is meditation, for God's Gaze to come into you is meditation, to speak His Speech is meditation, to inhale His Fragrance is meditation, to hear and enjoy His Sound is meditation, to hear the Resonance of His Heart and to resonate with that is meditation. Wisdom and these Qualities are needed.

My children, who are the gems of my eyes, you are trying to obtain peace, but you have forgotten the Commandments of God, you have forgotten your True Qualities, you have forgotten Who feeds you, Who gives you breath, and Who gives you life. You have forgotten the way God protects you, you have forgotten the way God feeds you.

My children, who are the gems of my eyes, God did not create one seed, He created many seeds. It is not something that the "I" can do. You may have a farm, you may even have this whole American continent, you may have the European continent, you may have the Asian continent, or you may have the whole African continent. You may rule these eight directions, you may do many things, but God is the One who creates many fruits out of one seed. Out of one seed He creates many seeds, but that seed is in the Hands of God. He multiplies these seeds, He makes them grow. He multiplies one into a thousand, ten thousand, or a hundred thousand.

By doing what you are now doing, your stomach will never be filled. The crops of those seeds are for your desire; they cannot fill your stomach. It is like hay—it cannot fill your stomach. That Seed which is in the Hands of God, that tiny Seed of Grace, He has kept within Himself. He has kept it within His Own Hand. What He has enlarged into ten thousand or into ten million is for your elements, for your five elements, for your body, for the mind and desire, for illusion, for the desire of the dog in your body, for the monkey of the mind, for the donkey, the goat, the bull, the lions, the tigers, the bears, for satan, for hell, for the fire of hell. These are the things He multiplied and gave you.

But He has kept one point with Himself. To man He has given one point. That point is His *Rahmat*, His Grace. That is the Seed. When Solomon, the son of David, tried to feed the fish in the ocean he could not even feed that one fish. He had so many worlds of food, but he could not feed one fish; however, this one point which came from God filled the stomach of that fish. He has this one *Rahmat*, this one Grace in His Hand to purify your hearts, to satisfy your hunger, to change your fatigue and tiredness, to give you strength, to give vision to your eyes, to give you that smell, to give you Wisdom, to give you Love, and to give you His Divine Qualities. This is that food. If this comes and falls into your mouth, it is the thing which will give satisfaction and remove your hunger and your fatigue. Please think about it. My children, who are the gems of my eyes, in this State God preached to Solomon, the son of David.

The people who live on the continents of America, Europe, and Africa are thinking, "We are growing food to feed the people of the world." One seed multiplies into several seeds. With these they are trying to feed the people of the world, but this is really hay. This hay will never satisfy the hunger of the stomach. God gives this hay, too, but it is for the donkey, for the horse, and for the bull. This is what He gives. He multiplies one into thousands. To whom is that given? It is given to the dog, to the foxes, to the demons, to the ghosts, and to the horses.

To Man, the Son of God, to Man's faith, to his love, to his intentions, to his qualities, to his actions, to his faith, to his determination, and to his thoughts of our Father, He gives His Food. That Food is His Love. It is Grace. It is *Imān*. That Food is the Food that will satisfy hunger. That is the Food for Man. It is the thing which gives him Wisdom. That Food will give him the Grace of God, it will give him the Wealth of God, it will give Undiminishing Bliss, it will give him Peace, it will give him Happiness, it will give the Light which protects him from the evils of satan, it will give the Light which can dispel all darkness and develop God's Qualities and the Wealth of His Grace. That Food will give Happiness, Bliss, and Heaven. The place in which he dwells will be the Kingdom of God, the place in which he lives will be the Kingdom of God, the place to which he goes will be the Kingdom of God; wherever he moves will be the Kingdom of God. For the one who attains this State, wherever he is will be Heaven. Think about this, children.

You have studied science, many books, psychology, and so many other things. That is very good, but you have to look at the Dictionary which God has given you. That Dictionary is within you. You also have to reach this Peace. Instead of this, however, you are trying to find some other kind of peace. True Peace is this Food from God. To Man, True Peace is this. Beasts can never reach that State of Peace or Tranquility, they will never reach that State of Peace. If Man perceives this True State, that is Peace.

Children, who are the gems of my eyes, since 1945 you think you have found a way to attain peace. You are trying to find peace of mind. Now you have also found a way to feed the people of the world. In this state you are reciting *mantras*, *tantras*, and meditations. You have forgotten the words of the prophets, you have forgotten the Commandments of God, the words of the prophets, Divine Justice, the King's Justice, Human Justice, and the Human Conscience. You have forgotten these types of Justice. Having forgotten them, you are trying to find some new way to be happy.

How are you searching for this happiness? You are searching for it through *sariyai, kiriyai, yogam*, and *gnānam* [the four steps in spiritual development]. You are searching for it through four hundred trillion, ten thousand different kinds of *mantras*. You are searching for it through different kinds of forces, you are searching for it through different types of magic and through different types of witchcraft; you are searching for it through different types of ghosts, demons, and through the meditations of devils; you are searching for it through miracles, you are searching for it through the 64 types of yogic meditation (meditation on the 64 types of sensual arts).

These kinds of meditations are like waves of the mind. You have been practicing these kinds of meditations. As a result of these you take marijuana, intoxicants, LSD, opium, and so many tens of millions of things which torporize your judgment. With these things you are trying to find peace of mind. You are reciting *mantras*. You say *aum, aam, eee, sam, zoom, beem, kam, poom, aaaa, eeeee, oooo, aai, ee.* You pay money. You try to recite these *mantras* and these meditations. You have given your mind trying to attain peace of mind.

You have been learning many things since 1945, but what is the peace you have found? The only thing you have done is to forget God. You have forgotten all the religions; you have forgotten the truth of the religions. But even though you have forgotten them, there is a section inside the religions. The Qualities of God are inside those religions, the Justice of God is inside those religions, the Truth of God is inside. Because there is Justice inside the religions there can be no business for them. Think about this with your Wisdom. You should look at the Truth of those religions, you should look at the Truth which the prophets brought. You should look at the Truth of God!

But you have given up the religions, you have given up the church, you have given up the mosque, you have given up all these things. In their place you have taken the *mantras* of satan, the forces of satan, the sun, the moon, and the stars. You have taken these demons, these ghosts, and these vampires into yourselves. You have all these in your mind and you have started to meditate on them! You have forgotten good conduct, good qualities, good thought— everything has been forgotten.

We have come to a state in which we do not even have the wisdom of beasts! Even a snake turns around three times before it rests. When it turns around three times, it meditates on God, saying, "My God." You will see that, before it sits, it turns around three times and says, "O my God, protect me." Look at the bull—even the bull turns around three times and says this. The horse does the same thing. Even the birds move themselves three times. The cock moves three times, raises its head, and then sleeps. All the beasts meditate on God before they sleep. What does man do? He meditates on satan and then goes to sleep. Having meditated on satan, on *māya*, on his elements, on his desires, on the monkey mind, on the horses, and on the donkey, he tries to attain peace.

Since 1945 these practices have increased tremendously. If you ask the reason, they will say they are trying to find peace. As a result of this, states have changed, ways have changed, religions have changed, kingdoms have changed, and the people of the country have changed. Even the body has become a slave now. You have forgotten Truth, you have forgotten Human Justice, and you have forgotten Human Conscience. Now you have satan as your helper. What is happening because of that? Poverty has come. You meditate so that you may become rich. You say *aaai, uuu, eee* to get rid of your diseases—you cannot get rid of those diseases this way. You want to become very rich, but you have no oil, your farm products are diminished. There are more rains coming, there are many earthquakes occuring; destruction is coming through gales; all the things which you are bringing up will be destroyed. Your business and income are decreasing; prices are increasing—the price of each product has multiplied ten times. A rich man has to become poor, a poor man has to become a beggar. The idea of murder has come into your meditation. There is a need to take more intoxicants. Many quarrels and problems have arisen. All the qualities of fear, bashfulness, shyness, modesty, and good qualities have disappeared. In all kingdoms murder and sin prevail. Each person is apparently trying to fight with the other.

Each person's strength has weakened. Now everyone has high blood pressure, evil diseases, diabetes, diseases of the eye, diseases of the blood, and heart troubles. All these diseases have increased. You say that you are trying to reach peace. Where is this peace? You are only increasing these illnesses. Because of all the meditations you have done since 1945—giving all your money—one hundred twenty-five dollars, two hundred dollars, and thousand dollars, one hundred thousand dollars, and shouting *aa, ee, iin, oom, oom, aaaa,* and *mmmmmm*—you have definitely forgotten God. As a result, the world has come to this state of destruction today. The seasons have changed, the rains have changed, the winds have changed, and the snow has changed. All your farming has changed. These things are all changing.

You have to think about the reasons for this. Think about the scientific investigations you have done. You may learn everything—you may learn all the sciences. With all of that, who reaches this peace? All the animals have reached this state of peace, the birds have reached this state of peace—even the geese, knowing the times and seasons, fly in various directions. But man has not understood time and season; he does not understand his wealth and his treasure. Man has not opened his dictionary and studied it. Man has not understood who he is. He has changed into another form. His stomach is never satisfied. He is trying to find peace of mind.

This is not the way to tranquilize your mind. It is like somebody trying to extinguish a fire with fire. He tries to put out a fire by using another fire. How can you blow out one fire by using another fire? This is the work of an idiot—only an idiot will try to blow out a fire by using another fire. The fire will only increase. The mind itself is a monkey. You are trying to meditate on the mind with the mind. That will kill you. It will destroy you. It will also destroy the entire world. You are trying to use water to build the shores of the ocean. When the water and the sea come together, the whole world will be flooded. You cannot build shores with water. You are using satan in trying to reach peace and tranquility of mind.

You have to pray in Truth. You have to meditate in Truth. You have to bring this mind into Peace. To do this you have to imbibe the Qualities of God, the Actions of

God, the Compassion of God, and the Love of God. You have to have His Faith, you have to have His Certitude, you have to have Certitude in His Laws. To do this you must have Wisdom. Only Wisdom will prevent this destruction. For forty-five minutes you meditate, reciting *aaa, eee, mmm.* This is not going to give you Peace. It is going to kill you and it is going to destroy this world! You are continually increasing such destruction.

Believe in the words of Jesus. Look inside the words of Jesus. Look inside the words of Moses. Look at the words of Jacob. Look inside the words of Muhammad. Look at the words of Abraham and look inside them. Look at the words Job said and look inside them. Satan did many evil things to Job. Was he able to do anything to the Peace which Job had? God gave Job that Tranquility and Peace. God is the One Who Protects. You must have that Certitude.

When Abraham was thrown into the fire, who helped him? Who could help him? The angel Michael and the angel Gabriel came to him. They wanted to know what help they could give to Abraham. The angel of wind, *Isrāfīl*, came to him and asked. "What help can I give you, O Abraham?" Then the angel of death, *'Izrā'eel*, came to him and said, "What help can I give you, O Abraham?" Abraham replied, "I do not need your help. I seek the help of the One who put me into this fire." This is the Certitude you must have. So God told His angels, "Abraham was seeking only My help."

You are looking for satan's help and asking for help from *maya* or illusion. What peace are you asking for? You want to have a lot of love; you want to have two or three or four kinds of love. You want to have a lot of sex. You want to make your body strong. If there is a disease, you may try to cure it. Then you make love and you have sex. This is a shame. This is such a pity.

If you are a True Human Being you must have Human Wisdom. The destruction of the world is near. Therefore, even now, try to develop faith in God. To have faith in God is meditation, to reflect on God is meditation, to intend God is meditation, and to keep this intention within your heart is meditation, to understand Wisdom and how to develop this Wisdom is meditation. Not meditating in this way is a sign of destruction. Each society is trying to collect more and more people so that they may live in peace. Who is in a state of peace? You will never be in a state of peace. That kind of peace is a sign of destruction.

Mind is illusion. It has waves. If you can still that mind for one second, you can reach God. If you can still or control that mind and control these five senses for one second, you can reach God. Only if you have faith in God, only if you have the Qualities of God and the Intention of God can you reach the State of God. Do not do the meditation of the monkeys, the meditation of the dogs, the meditations of the cats, the meditations of the rats, the meditation of the elephants, the meditation of the beasts, or the meditation of satan. This can only result in destruction.

Therefore, my children, please think about this. Reflect on it. Prayer to God is Good Thoughts, prayer to God is Good Conduct, prayer to God is His Good Qualities, prayer to God is His Good Actions, prayer to God is to reflect and to know God, prayer to God is to have His Beauty, prayer to God is to have His Looks, prayer to God is to develop His Wisdom. Understanding these things is our work.

My children, the day of destruction is very near.

Therefore, do not collect people and give two hundred or two hundred and fifty dollars so that this destruction can come faster. Do not increase this business, because through it comes destruction. In this world, to find one person in ten million meditating on God is rare. You are tryng to increase the majority. But the majority will go to hell. It is difficult to find one person in ten million who exists in Truth. According to what the Bible and the Qur'an said, and according to what Jesus said, during the time of the destruction of this world people will follow satan, his qualities, his prayer, and his meditation which is the love of hell and *māya*. These things will take place at the time of the end of the world: there will be poverty, famine, difficulties, contagious diseases, new diseases, distresses, poverty, battles, fights, murder between husbands and wives, and murder between children and parents. There will be intoxicants. All of the qualities of beasts will come into man. The satanic qualities will come into man. The satanic qualities will come into man. Because of that they will accept satan.

They will not accept True Man and the Truth. The Bible and the Qur'an have shown these things. Jesus, Abraham, Moses, and the other prophets have predicted them. That time is now. There are very few True Men. There are human beings, but they have changed. Animals have not changed, but men have changed into beasts. Our thoughts and our meditations have changed into beasts. All of our actions have changed into bestial qualities. This is the time of destruction.

The forces of destruction arise from *mantras*, magics, demons, illusion, and satan. As a result many difficulties will come, and destruction will follow. There will be many gales, the oceans will swell and overflow, there will be many winds, there will be earthquakes, and there will be volcanoes. Crops will diminish, the vision of the eye will diminish, wisdom will diminish, life and age will also diminish. People will be sinners.

God says: "O My slaves, please escape. Those who have accepted Me in Truth, please escape. Destruction will occur through atomic explosions, through fights, battles, and weapons, through poisons and poisonous snakes, and through mountains of fire. O My slaves, those who have accepted My Words and the words of My prophets, do not get entangled in the nets of satan, do not pray to satan, do not listen to the words of satan, do not recite the *mantras* of satan, do not keep satan in your hearts! Live like children of God and keep only God in your hearts. There is only a short time to go. There will be only very few such people, and they will be very rare. Those who accept Me will be very few, even one in ten million is rare. During this time of destruction, I will protect those who have accepted Me."

God says this: "Whatever the others grow within them, whatever they nurture within them as a result of that, I will make them die. They will perish as a result of the things they have acquired. Difficulties will arise." This is what God and the prophets have said. These explanations have been given. That period of time is very close.

Within the last ten or fifteen years America has changed. Everyone knows *mantras*. Everyone does business. Everyone says *oom* and *aam, aamm, oom, aaa, eee, aaaa,* and *mmmm.* Now this has become a big business. But it has no meaning; it has no relationship to anything. There is no meaning in it. *Ah, ee, aa* is not even a *mantra.* Please think about this. Think about this and change now!

If one child out of ten million acquires that Wisdom and tries to worship our Father, then the gales which come may be less severe. Universities are crazy about *mantras* and the worship of demons and satan. There are universities which worship dogs, and there are universities which worship cats, and there are universities which cause destruction.

O my children, who are the most wonderful children, there are two hundred million Americans in this country. If twenty of you can come, if you can come towards God, you can stop all this destruction and all these difficulties. If twenty of you can become True Human Beings and exist as True Human Beings and accept God, it will be very good. This is my word to you. The prophets have said this before, and I am saying this now. The prophets said it before—whether we understood them or not; now I am saying the same thing. Destruction is very close. Each of us is starting a fire of *māya* within. We have become the firewood to hell. In this state we are trying to find peace. How is this going to end? The same fire is going to burn us. It is going to destroy us. Therefore, please think.

Out of the two hundred million people in America, it is very difficult for even twenty of them to come forward to pray to God and to realize Him. If you reach that Good State, then all the gales which may come will be prevented. If one child becomes a child of God, it will be like a huge mountain, a mountain much bigger than Mount Sinai. That mountain will prevent all the storms. If there are twenty children who are like twenty mountains, then all this famine and distress will be stopped. Please accept the Path of God in Truth and strive hard on it so that we may escape this destruction. Please try to reach this State.

Search for Peace in the Place of God. Try to know who you are. Try to find Peace in God. If you imbibe the Qualities of God, you will have that Peace. Do not waste forty-five minutes every day like this. You can reach your Father in two minutes if you can be still. If you can close your eyes for two minutes and reflect on God, that will be enough. If you can think about God for even four minutes, then you can reach God and that Station of Peace.

My children, please try. Do not keep looking at this world. Look at yourselves. Try to correct yourselves. You have certain treasures, you have this Dictionary within you. God's Dictionary is within you, but you need Wisdom in order to understand it. You must know the languages in order to understand it. Please try to escape. Even if only a few escape, it will be very good.

My children, who are the gems of my eyes, this is the thing which will get rid of all your poverty and famine. This is the thing which will get rid of all your famine. These *mantras* cannot create peace. They only destroy peace. They cause more distress and more problems. Please do not do this. Please search for the Truth. My children, think about this. Try to find your Wisdom, the Beauty of God, His Qualities, and the inner meanings of what the prophets have said. Please try to understand that. Look hard and deeply into that and try to understand it. That will be very good. Then we can escape. My love. My greetings.

The Mind

Children, gems of my eyes, in this world we have to reflect. Children, gems of my eyes, this world is a great, expansive thing. In everyone's life this world is the mind. This mind is the world. This mind is a huge world. This body is a secret, and this mind is a secret. For man to transcend and go beyond these is rare. However, you, we, everyone must reflect—this mind and this secret body are always liable to accidents. Everywhere we look, accidents are lurking. Everywhere we go, there are accidents. Wherever the eye and the body look, there is an accident.

The mind is a thing that flies around the skies. The mind has tens of millions of qualities. The mind has tens of millions of shadows. The mind has tens of millions of shapes. The mind has tens of millions of colors. The mind has tens of millions of darknesses. The mind has tens of millions of vapors and winds. The mind has tens of millions of diseases. The mind has tens and tens of millions of potential qualities and pranks. The mind has tens of millions of monkey forms. The mind has 1,008 kinds of snake-like qualities. The mind has the quality of demons. The mind has the qualities of *maya* [illusion]. The mind has the qualities of ghosts. The mind has the qualities of angels. The mind has the qualities of darkness. The mind has the qualities of birds. (It flies around.) The mind has the qualities of shadows. The mind has the connection with ether or space. The mind flies around the ether and space. The mind has tens of millions of connections of rebirths. The mind has the ties of earth. The mind has the ties of fire. The mind has the ties of water. The mind has the ties of many births. The mind has tens of millions of dog-like connections. The mind has the ties of desires. The mind has the ties of craving. The mind has limitless ties of blood connections. The mind has the ties of sex. The mind has the ties of torpor. The mind has the ties of turmoils. The mind has the ties of differences. The mind has the ties of arrogance. The mind has the ties of ignorance. The mind has the ties of *karma* [the inherited properties formed at the time of conception]. The mind has the ties of *maya*. The mind has the ties of filth. Like this, the mind—our mind—has an infinite number of ties.

This mind, this embryo, and these connections take shape when the body forms. The *karmic* ties of the qualities of the mother and father, the qualities of the earth, the qualities of the thoughts of our mother and father, the qualities of their blood and its ties, the ties of their arrogance, the ties of water, fire, and food, and many other such ties take shape. The connections that are transmitted from the mother and the father to the foetus are many. These connections did not exist in the original egg, but tens of millions of *karmic* connections have collected in the blood, in the lymph, and in the flesh. From their qualities and from the qualities of the minds of both parents come those ties such as happiness and sorrows, sadness and turmoils, torpor and darkness, fights and quarrels. Like this, there are many ties which exist as the ties of conception. And what was formed out of all these ties is the mind.

The ties contained within the mind and its state are limitless. Many strengths exist within this mind. When this foetus was formed, good actions and bad actions, good and evil, hell and heaven, truth and falsehood, darkness and light, right and wrong, purity and impurity, love and sadness, patience and anger, sadness and happiness—all these qualities came and filled the mind. This mind, which contains all these strengths and *saktis* [forces or energies], is a baby—a baby mind, a monkey mind, a dark mind, an ether mind, a mind of the elements. Since it has all these states, it has a lot of might and strength. Therefore, no one can calm the mind. How can we control this mind and achieve tranquility and peace with these things that cannot cause peace? We must reflect on this a little. The world has taken over this mind and is in search of peace, but this can never be done.

When the foetus is conceived and formed, the fertilized ovum is jailed in the prison of the tubes for the first three days. After that, for nine months it is imprisoned in the dark prison of the womb. After nine months, when the tenth month dawns, the infant now frees himself from that dark prison. Once he is freed from the dark cave of the womb, his parents and his relatives carry him, wash him, clean him, and keep him in the prison of their laps. They keep him enclosed in their laps, not giving him the freedom to go here or there. Later on he is imprisoned in

31

the jail of his cot. Still later he is imprisoned in the lap of his nurse. So for one or two years he is in the jailhouse of his cot, the lap of his parents, and the lap of his nurse. After that he enters the prison of school. Each grade of study is a prison to him. When he leaves grade school he enters the jailhouse of college. He leaves that jailhouse and enters the jailhouse of jobs. Then he enters the jailhouse of marriage. Later he enters the jailhouse of his wife. Then he enters the jailhouse of his children. Later he enters the jailhouse of disease. Still later he enters the jailhouse of good and bad. Later he enters the jailhouse of wealth and poverty. During all of this, the jailhouse is his life. Finally he enters the jailhouse of death. And after death he enters the jailhouse of either good or bad actions.

In this state the mind experiences sadness and happiness, richness or poverty, and one's entire life is spent in this jail or prison house. Not for one day, not for one second, does he ever live free of a jailhouse, keeping himself in this state of continuous imprisonment.

For the sake of our body or for the sake of our wealth, we have nurtured this thing which is liable to accidents. We are doing this for the sake of our body, for money, sex, and happiness. We are also trying to meditate without ever freeing ourselves from this prison. It is not possible for one who is in the jailhouse to reach the state of peace or tranquility. Is this not so? Please think. Our whole life is a prison. We have been in this prison from the time we appeared in the dark cave of the womb and throughout our entire life.

Some, while living within these prisons, are trying to find peace. Some, by trying to accumulate money, are trying to find peace. Some, by getting married, are hoping to find peace. Some are taking drugs and trying to find peace. Some drink whiskey, beer, and brandy, and try to find peace. They are searching for peace of mind. Some are trying to reach peace by meditating. Some do *yoga* and try to reach peace. Some try to reach peace through *gnānam* [wisdom], by reciting *mantras*, or by this or that. Some do *pūjas* [ritual offerings] and try to reach peace. Some donate their wealth and try to reach peace. Like this, in many ways they are searching for peace.

But we have to reflect. Through what can we reach real Peace? What is that Treasure that can give us Peace? We must first search for the path of freedom to escape from the jailhouse where we are imprisoned. What is it that can bring about real Peace in our life?

Without knowing this, the world has discovered a 'new way' to reach 'peace of mind'. Since the end of the Second World War, for the sake of money and business, the world has discovered new forms of meditations. By meditation they have caught hold of 'peace of mind'. The world, in these new and different ways of meditation, has a 'new way'.

God's Laws, Human Conscience, Justice, Truthfulness, Patience, Serenity, Kindness, and Duty—these states have been forgotten, and man has discovered new ways of meditation, a new way of peace. While living in the prisons and the jailhouses, they still call it 'peace'. You can never reach real Peace in this way.

If you want to reach Peace, then you must reflect a little. If Peace is needed, then first free yourself from the jailhouse. Please think about this. If you want Peace, then you must think about what Treasure can give you that Peace. What is Peace? The one who wants to attain Peace of Mind must free himself from the jailhouse. Our life is fully immersed in accidents, in jail. Our thoughts, our sight, our sounds, our ears—all these form our prison.

The prison of religion, the prison of race, the prison of castes, the prison of ties to blood relatives, the prison of wealth, the prison of desire, the prison of love, the prison of this body—all these are prisons. It is only when we free ourselves from these prisons that we will reach Peace or *Shānti*—Peace of Mind.

The mind contains all these things. The one who keeps all this, who locks the doors, closes the house, climbs a tree, stands on the head and raises the feet above, closes the eyes, sits in cross-legged positions, holds the breath, closes the mouth, closes the eyes, and, like this, does so many forms of physical exercises, may do so. But to be imprisoned, and to reach Peace while still being imprisoned, is extremely difficult. Please reflect. The world is searching for peace. If you can reflect and think awhile about the ways to attain peace, there is a simple way. We must think about what this simple way is.

Whatever we yearn for becomes our prison. We have to find freedom by removing that same thing.

That is, there is the One who created us. He must be present. He is that One Treasure that nurtures us. He is that One Truth. We must understand this Truth, and through the knowledge of this Truth, we must become free from our attachments and this jailhouse. Then there is Peace. That is easy.

The thing we saw once, we now desire to see again. What did we see first? What did we see when we came into this world? What is it that we desire to see again? You must reflect upon this.

This mind, this eye, this desire, this nose, this ear—reflect deeply upon them. Then think about the passage that we came through and what it is that we desire to see again—we must think. If we think this over, then we may be able to find a way to Peace of Mind. We saw something when we came to this world, now we desire to see this again. What is it that we saw earlier, and what is it that we wish to see again?

The passage through which we came, our place of birth, our jailhouse, that dark room of the womb, how we escaped from it—if we reflect a little about that, we will understand a little about going back to the prison again. If we understand that, then Peace will come. Why did we enter that dark cave? How did our form appear in that dark cave? What parts went to make our form? Earth, fire, water, air, and ether compose this form. How did man enter that cave, and with what ties did he get there? We entered through the ties of arrogance, *karma*, and *māya*. What happened to these eight parts? What turned them into this prison?

This mind is the cause. We must reflect upon this. The thing that entered that cave was imprisoned for ten months. Then it left that cave and came out. Having come out, we are still dwelling in that prison. What is that thing? Why is it trying to re-enter that cave? Why is the mind trying to return there? What is the reason for its re-entry? You must reflect upon this with your wisdom—with the wisdom of your feeling, awareness, intellect, judgment, Wisdom, and Divine Analytic Wisdom.

With your Divine Analytic Wisdom, analyze and find that Path which will give you Peace. That Path will be revealed to you. If that Path, that Way to reach Peace, is known and realized, you will say, "Oh, this is the Path to Peace." Once you see that Path to Peace, you will say, "Oh, this is the Path to Peace." Once we know this Path, we realize and understand that this mind, which does so many tens and tens of millions of things, can never be made peaceful. Then we begin to think, "What is that which is needed to give this mind Peace?"

We need not be in prison every day. We should think about this. We must realize and understand this, that we must give something to this monkey, this baby who keeps everything and plays with it. What should we place before it? We must give this baby a new toy. It has to be a toy that this baby has never seen before. All the toys in the market are things with which the baby keeps on playing. Still, if it sees something new, it will ask for it. Then if it sees another thing, it will ask for that. When it sees still another thing in the market, it will ask for that. We keep on carrying this baby all the time. We are keeping this monkey with us all the time, and we are holding this dog all the time. We are carrying the monkey, the baby, and the dog. We are taking these three with us so they may help us. Wherever we may go these three things will come with us. Of these three things, one is a baby and the second is the dog of desire. This dog of desire will always want those things that are dirty and filthy—even feces. It will smell these things and drag you along with it. It will keep on dragging you. It is a big dog, like an Alsatian. The dog will keep on howling and howling, "Hooo! hooo!" Because of its strength, it pulls you in its direction, and you keep following it.

Next, whatever the baby sees in the market, whatever things it sees, it keeps on crying and says, "Give me this, give me that, give me this!" So when you buy it one thing, it plays for awhile, discards it, and demands another thing. Like this, it keeps on demanding everything it sees. That baby has no peace whatsoever. It keeps on crying all the time.

While this is so, that monkey—that monkey of the mind which is equivalent to 70 battalions of monkeys—when it sees a tree it jumps. When it sees a fruit it jumps. When it sees a branch it jumps. When it sees a leaf it jumps. When it sees the trees in the jungles—whatever scenes it sees—it jumps. It takes the form of the universe, it jumps, and it leaps.

Because of this, if you carry these three things with you, how can you hope to reach Peace? To merely talk about peace is easy. Perhaps you are just talking about this. By closing the door and chanting, *aiing*, or by chanting *ommm*, or by saying *aummmmm*, or whatever you may chant, these three things will never leave you. You may recite these chants after closing the door or after closing your eyes. Even if you stand on your head and recite these, and even if you fold up your body and recite these—in whatever manner you recite these chants, whether hidden in a cave or hidden in the darkness—these three things will still stay with you. The monkey will jump, the baby will cry, and the dog will pull you. My children, who are the gems within my eyes, in this world you must reflect. If you keep these three things with you, how are you ever going to meditate? *Aiing, aiing.* These are just wasteful words. This is business work. This is a new technique of meditation. You all have found this new technique. Since 1944, you have found many new techniques of meditation, new techniques of prayers and new techniques to reach 'peace'. But this is not Peace.

Having understood these three sections, beat up that dog who keeps demanding this and that, and tie it up. Tie it behind the kitchen with a strong chain. Don't carry it in your hands. Feed it when it is hungry. This baby will keep on crying all the time. The monkey must be chained under a tree, the tree of Faith. This dog of desire must be tied behind the kitchen and must be taught patience. When it barks, say, "Have patience! I will give it to you. Wait, wait." For the baby, buy it something good and give it to it. There is nothing in the market of this world that the baby has not seen. There is no market that the mind has not seen. The mind has seen everything, and it keeps searching and running, and it keeps on discarding. So it throws away what it had, then it cries. Then it holds onto something, then it throws it away again, then it cries again. Then it smiles, and then it discards it.

Therefore, for that baby, which is the mind that keeps on flying between the earth and the sky, you have to find a thing that it has never seen. If you want Peace, then you have to find this thing. That thing which the mind has not seen is the Truth. That thing which the mind has not seen is Wisdom. That thing which the mind has not seen is God. That thing which the mind has not seen is Light. That thing which the mind has not seen is Eternal Bliss. That Light, that Plenitude, that thing which the mind has not seen is that Wealth of Bliss. That Wealth is very, very beautiful. It has Great Light, Great Power, and Great Bliss. It is not possible to describe all this. This is that Treasure that the baby mind, the dog of desire, and the monkey of the mind have never seen.

You must think about this Treasure if you want Peace. If you want Peace of Mind, if you want freedom from the jailhouse, if you want to escape from this dog of desire, if you want to run away from the monkey of the mind, and if you want to reach the state of Peacefulness, there is an easy way. You have to implant the state of Compassionate Love in your heart. You have to fix the Seat of God's

Justice in your heart. You have to fix the Qualities of God in your heart. You have to fix the Actions of God in your heart. You must reflect over God in your heart. Those thoughts will give you Peace. Those ideas will give you Peace. Those looks will give you Peace. That State is like a palace that can give you Peace of Mind. It is a priceless Treasure. It is a Peaceful Treasure. It can give Peace or *Shānti*. In the world, the world of vision, in the world of thoughts and memories, in the world of dreams, in the world of Wisdom, in the world of Souls, in the world of *Gnānam*, in the world of our Father, our God, in that world of Plenitude, in the world of Complete Light, it will give you Peace. In all of these worlds it will grant you Peace.

Instead of this however, for many years you have been spending forty-five minutes, an hour, four hours, or five hours a day in search of peace by using new techniques. If you want Peace, give up these techniques and still your *mind* for ten minutes, for twenty minutes, or for even five minutes. Please think about this. Think deeply about this.

Do this with *Īmān*—with absolute and complete Faith, Certitude of Belief, Determination to realize God, and Wisdom. Having thought about this with your Wisdom, please look into your heart and reflect over this thought. Sit down, and for ten minutes, recite these two words in your heart: *Lā Ilāha*. (Other than You there is nothing.) *Ill Allāhu*. (You are God.) Other than You there is no God. You are God. You are God. There is no other God than You. Say this within the depths of your heart. Say it for twenty minutes or ten minutes or five minutes, by sitting in one place, focusing your attention on the heart, and saying it with determination. Please say it in the mornings, in the evenings, or before you eat, for even five minutes.

Looking within your heart with determination and

concentration, the more you go on reciting this *Kalimah*, the more you will begin to experience so much bliss. You will see a great light there. You will see paradise there. You will see a large palace there. You will see a large blissful house there. You will see an immense light. You will see the heavenly maidens there. You will see a large flower garden there. You will see a large fruit orchard there. You will see an immense river there. You will see a magnificent ocean of milk there. You will see a huge river of honey there. You will see the Grace which will give you bliss and cause you to be intoxicated. You will see a large palace seven stories high. You will see heaps and heaps of silver, gold, and pure gold used for decorations. You will see heaven's large palace, which is eight stories high. You will see the house where you are going to live. There you will be able to experience the bliss that belongs to your *Shaikh*—your Guru. You will see the maidens of heaven inviting you. You will see heavenly angels that will take you around. You will see the angels inviting you. You will see the section where *Munkar* and *Nakir* [the two angels who inquire at the grave, concerning good and evil] are, and where judgment takes place. You will see the beginning and the end. You will see many, many beings there.

As you recite this *Kalimah* more and more, you will experience more and more bliss. You will see things flying. You will see things going. You will go there and see that Light. You will go within and see. You will see the seven heavens open up. You will see the crossing of the seven worlds. You will see that which transcends *māya* and goes within. As you go further and further within your heart, you will see wonder after wonder after wonder. You will see honey come into your mouth, and you will experience the taste of it without eating it. You will taste the deli-

40

ciousness of fruit that has come into your mouth without plucking it. You will see the fruit smile, then come to your mouth; it will even squeeze the juice into your mouth. You will see food come into your mouth before you can intend it. Whatever food you may want will come like that. Whatever service you may need will be done before you can think about it. Before you can even think about it, you will be lifted and carried to places you need to go. You will see 'alam [the world], arwāh [the hereafter], and all of everything there. You will see the eight heavens. You will see the seven hells. You will see all the wonders that are happening there. You will hear the Sounds and the Secrets of God. You will hear the Bliss of God. You will hear the Resonance of God. You will see the Light of God. You can see all the wonders there. Like this, when you are witnessing this bliss, and while you are reciting this Word—this Kalimah—which must become deeply impressed within your heart, that house will be opened. The bliss that you experience when that house is opened will give you Peace of Mind. It is from that bliss that you can achieve Peace.

Once this baby has seen and seen this bliss, it will say, "Ah, ah, ah! What bliss this is ! What bliss this is! Is there more bliss than this?" Then the baby will go to sleep. The mind will become entranced. The mind will just go to sleep. Everyday that the mind looks at this, it will experience bliss. Everyday that the mind looks at this, it will say, "That is good! That is so good!" You will go on increasing the amount of time that you spend reciting this Word, first ten minutes, then twenty minutes, then twenty-five minutes, thirty minutes, thirty-five minutes, then forty minutes. And as you experience so much bliss, you will keep on saying this more and more. You will keep on thinking and thinking of this and saying this Word. This Word is what will give you Peace.

Once you have crossed this path, you will be shown the secrets of the three worlds. You will be shown bliss, and it will make you understand. This State is bliss. If you achieve this State, this is Peace of Mind.

My children, the gems of my eyes, please make this State firm. This is Meditation. This is what will give you Peace of Mind. This is what will give Peacefulness to the mind. This is the Path through which the mind can become enamored. This Path existed then, and it exists now. (But we have given that up and we are holding a 'new method' in our hands.) That Way appeared at the time when Adam appeared and it continues to be that Way.

But man has forsaken that Way. He is holding onto the world but has forsaken the Truth. He has forsaken the Truth, and that is what is wrong. It is not God who has forsaken us and made us suffer! That potential to achieve Peace exists now and has always existed. If what has been given up or forsaken is taken back into the hands again, Peace will be achieved. Peace of Mind will be achieved.

When that Peace of Mind is achieved, it will give everything. It will give good benefits. It will give money. It will cure the 4,448 diseases of the nerves. It will remove the 84 kinds of diseases caused by air. It will cure the diseases of *karma*. It will cure the disease of illusion. It will cure the diseases of arrogance. It will cure the 21 diseases of the eyes caused by things that cover the eyes. It will cure all the diseases of the eyes, and it will give vision. It will increase the vision of the eyes. It will make the eyes clear, it will relieve the pain of the eyes, it will remove the things which cover the eyes, and it will give peace in that way. It will cure the 18 kinds of sinus diseases. It will cure the 18 types of rectal diseases, like bleeding hemorrhoids, prolapsed hemorrhoids, and all the diseases associated with the rectum. It will cure all the diseases of the urine, like sugar in the urine. It will cure headaches, dizziness, torpor, and suffering. It will cure the 96 madnesses. It will cure oozing diseases. It will cure diseases of the skin. It will cure eczema. It will cure diseases of the flesh. It will cure diseases of the marrow. It will cure all diseases. It will cure diseases of the nerves. It will cure diseases of the bones. It will cure the *karmic* diseases of man. It will cure exhaustion and tiredness. It will cure asthma. It will cure bronchitis. It will cure tuberculosis. It will cure cancer. Like this, it will cure so many, many diseases.

It will make you have a long life. It will make you look sixteen years old. It will bring beauty to you. It will bring beauty to your face. It will change your blood into the blood of a young child. The eyes will become the eyes of a young child. The skin will become the skin of a young child. The bones will become the bones of a young child. It will give you the qualities of a young child. It will give you the cells of a young child. It will give the bliss of a young child. When you continue meditation in this way, youthful qualities, youthful beauty, youthful light, and youthful color will be seen in you. In this state, these things will be experienced. Whatever you may want or need you will receive. You will get cash. You will receive money, and you will get peace. This is something that can give you everything. It will remove diseases, illnesses, poverty, difficulties, dangers, and accidents. It will remove all these things.

This is a State that existed before and that will always

exist. But man has forsaken this. If you establish this State again, you can achieve Peace. That is Peace.

Lā Ilāha. There is nothing other God. *Ill Allāhu,* You are God. If you say this for five, ten, or fifteen minutes, you can achieve that Peace of Mind. If you intend this in your heart with Faith, Certitude, and Determination, you can achieve Peace of Mind. You can close your eyes, or you can open your eyes, but you must look intently within your heart. Then you can achieve, whatever you intend. That Peace will come and the mind will go to sleep. It will go to sleep for a long time. Whatever you look at, your thoughts will be in heaven, in paradise with the heavenly beings and the angels. Whatever you intend with Faith will be seen as you go further and further within. It will be opened and you will see. The mind will just fall asleep. Desire will be destroyed. The monkey, having seen that Light, will become tired and weary. The monkey will become tired, desire will become dazzled, and the mind will become absorbed and entranced. It will have seen bliss. That State is Meditation.

If you want Peace, recite this *Kalimah.* This is the way to Peace of Mind. This is Peacefulness. This is heaven. This is life. This is bliss. This is destiny. If you want Peace, you must do this. This is very necessary for you. Of all the things that you can do in the world, you should do this. Every child should do this. This is Peace.

At that time [the time of creation] God gave the commandment to say this *Kalimah,* and now He wants you to say this. Of all things this is the best. It is because we have forsaken this that we are suffering. Do not forsake this. From now on recite this *Kalimah.* Through this you will attain Peace of Mind.

Ameen. Ameen. Ameen.

44

True Man

This is the way to attain Peace. You say that you want to achieve peace of mind. It seems that since 1944 you have discovered a 'new way' to achieve peace of mind. You say *om*, *am*, *eem*, *oh*, *aim*, *am*, *ahh*, *ee*, *mm*, and you pay two hundred and fifty dollars for that. You close your eyes and recite *ah*, *eem*, *mm*. You are trying to find peace of mind by saying these things. This is not peace of mind or tranquility; this is just a 'new way'.

God has given us Peace. In order for us to reach Peace, God has sent His messengers, His saints, and His prophets. There is a Beautiful Treasure which creates Peace within us. (It is not this 'new way'.) That Treasure appeared at the time of creation. Even today there is a place for that Treasure to give us peace of mind. It is the only thing which can give us peace of mind. (But *ah*, *ee*, *oo* is not that thing.) The place of peace of mind is the Point which comes from God. It exists even today, but man has forsaken that Point.

The animals are continuing to respond to the warnings that have been given to them, but man has turned into satan. Man has given up Wisdom. Having given up Wisdom, he is trying to find peace of mind. He is trying to find a new way to achieve peace of mind. Man has given up Wisdom, but the animals are living according to the rules and laws of God. They are in peace.

Since man has changed into satan, he is causing harm to animals. Man is causing harm to the animals and to the birds. Man has forgotten Peace and has changed into satan. Animals have not changed. They are always living in peace, they have a state of tranquility at all times. They eat and they are happy. They live in the rain, the sun, and the wind. No matter what comes, they do not feel any tiredness. They say, "My God," and they reflect upon God.

As soon as they see that dangerous man who has now changed into satan, they run away from him. The animals, the big birds, and the small birds all run away from him. They flee from him. The birds look at him and say, "This dangerous animal is coming!" And they fly away. They do this because man has changed from man to satan.

If there is a snake in a place where a cow is grazing, the snake will pass around the cow because it is not afraid of the cow. The cow grazes by itself, while the snake minds its own business and goes away. Animals live amicably with each other; but as soon as they see man, they run away. If we were True Men, the animals would not run away; but since we have become the most wicked of all wicked animals, when animals see us they become frightened and run away.

If animals see a True Man they will not run away. If they see a True Man, animals will come and pay obeisance to him, bowing their heads in front of him. Snakes, animals, and reptiles will pay their respects. If they see a man-animal, however, they will run away. If they see satan they will run. They will cry out and run away. The reason is that man has changed.

Now if we can change back to the True Form of Man, nothing will run away from us. Instead, they will perform their duty, they will all perform their duty. The reason they run away is because of the state that presently exists. But when you become True Man you will have Compassion. There will be Compassion in your look. When that Compassionate Love or Look falls upon animals, they will immediately return this love and say, "My Father!" When the Beauty of your Father is in your face, and when there is no scent of having killed any other beings, the animals will sense that, they will think that you are their Father, and they will pay obeisance to you.

The essence, smells, blood, and perspiration of whatever flesh you eat will come out through your own body and through your perspiration. That smell comes out through our own perspiration. If we eat beef, the smell of beef is emitted. If we eat beef, we receive the qualities of a cow. That smell is emitted through our skin, flesh, and blood. When a cow sees us, it can immediately scent the smell of a cow in us. It immediately thinks that this man is a tiger trying to attack it. It says, "Aiyo!" and runs away. Similarly, if we eat goat's flesh, the same thing happens. If we eat pig's flesh, the same thing will happen. The animals can scent this from our perspiration and from our bodies.

But if we have no scent of animal flesh, the animals immediately recognize us as "my Father." Because the

Fragrance of the Father is there, they can smell it. The Fragrance of God's Qualities is there. The Fragrance of God's Light is there. The Fragrance of God is there. As soon as they recognize that, the animals say, "My Father!" Then, in their own language they will call to you and pay obeisance to you. They will bow down and pay obeisance to you, and out of love they may even come and lick you. The reason is that you are True Man. If you become True Man, all animals will respect you. The Fragrance of Truth and the Qualities of God will be in you. Until that time, the qualities of whatever we use will be absorbed by us.

It is man, therefore, who has changed. He has changed into satan. He has changed into a beast. Since the smell of satan or the smell of a beast is there, the other animals look at him and run away. They do not run away from other animals, but they run when they see the animal-man. It is like this. Through our perception, our awareness, our intellect, and our Wisdom, we should try to change ourselves back into True Human Beings. We have to leave this animal form—this dangerous animal and satan—and become True Man again. That will be very good. Then all lives will respect you. You will be the Son of God, the Prince of God. All lives will pay obeisance to you. Darkness will leave you, illusion will run away, satan will run away when he sees you, and animals will pay obeisance to you. In that State there is True Peace of Mind.

If we erase the tape in which we were transformed from man to beast, or to satan, and if we can erase all the dangerous qualities and take in the original qualities that were there when we were born, then we will have no suffering. We will have no suffering. That is Peace of Mind. Then nothing will harm us. If we do not harm anything, nothing will harm us. That is what is called Peace of Mind, or Tranquility. Please do that. We must develop the Qualities of God, we must live and understand the Truth, we must worship that One, and we must live as one family. In this state we need to have Compassion, Love, Tolerance, and Peacefulness. This should be our life, our existence. It is through these Qualities that we can reach Peace of Mind. Having reached Peace, we can then understand how to pray to God. That will be very good.

But if, instead of that, you continue to create different kinds of societies and study all the scriptures and *vēdānta* [philosophy], what is the purpose? God is a Treasure which has transcended the limits of religions and philosophies, and which cannot be seen within them. Since God transcends religion and philosophies, another type of study is necessary to know Him. He exists beyond all this. He is Truth, Reality. God has no story, no book, no history; therefore, you must transcend and go beyond everything. You have to find some other way to realize that which has no history. We need the Qualities of God. We have to develop the Qualities of God, we have to develop the Actions of God, and we have to do the Duties of God. When we go beyond everything in searching for Him, the Qualities of God—that Justice—will be a Magnet. Then there will be Justice, Divine Justice.

You are the king of the kingdom of your heart. Taking Divine Justice you must place it within the king's justice. The body is a human being; therefore, you must take this king's justice and transform it into human justice. Then you must take human justice and place it in your human conscience. Then you have to take on the Qualities of God. Taking on the Qualities of God and expanding them is the Form of God.

49

You must begin to analyze God through His Form. You have to analyze God with His Magnetic Form. When you continue to look at that Form, when you look at the world with the Form of that Magnet, the Magnet will immediately be drawn to a particular point. The Power of God will pull this magnet into it. As it goes on pulling and pulling and pulling you in, you will finally be swallowed into that Power. That Power is God.

It is through God's Qualities that we have to see that Power. The State which is His Form is God's Qualities, God's Actions, God's Compassion, God's Love, God's Tolerance, God's Peacefulness, the treatment of all lives as one's own, Selfless Duty, and Duty without the 'you' and the 'I'. This State is His Form, and it is able to detect that Power. It is the Magnet which detects that Power. It does not harm any lives.

When these two get together, that Power will draw this Magnet into it and swallow it up. That is God. Then you can get inside God in order to research Him. You cannot search for Him through books, through religions, through pictures, through desires, or through the differences of religions. That Power is the Truthful Treasure which transcends all *vēdas* and *vēdāntas*. It transcends races, religions, and differences. That Powerful Thing is called God.

If we want to analyze God, we must have the Form of God within us. We can analyze God only through His Form. Both are One. That Form is also His Power. The Qualities of God are His Kingdom. The Form of that Kingdom is the Trustee. The Power of that Trustee is the Power of God. It is through this that you can search for God and find Him. Then you will become the Son of God and you will be in the station of Man-God. That is the reason this name is given.

My children, we have to search for God in this way. If we search with Wisdom, if we have Divine Qualities within us, and if we reach God, then we can realize Him. That will be good.

The Right and the Left

Bismillahirahmaniraheem.

May God help us all. All praise is to Allah.

My dear children, gems of my eyes, gems who are within my heart, the ripe fruits of my heart, who are my taste; children who have grown with the Compassion and Love of God, the princes of God; O jewels of my eyes, may God protect you all. In the three worlds may God protect you from all accidents. May He feed you with the milk of Love. *Ameen. Ameen. Ameen.*

Children, gems of my eyes, what you were told now is just a small point. There are many more things which I said in the earlier part of the night for this discourse. Those are the Secrets of God. The Secrets of God are within us. However, gems within my eyes, you have to reflect. The way the world is progressing now could lead to many accidents. There is a difference between the intentions and behavior in the world now. It is like the difference between the water that comes from the springs within the earth and the water that flows from a mountain top.

The water that flows down from the mountain top is from the rain, and there is a magnetic power within it. That rainwater has the property of giving life or making the herbs, the trees, and the weeds on which it falls to grow. It is an extremely subtle power. If the trees or the grass draw it, immediately they will have the power to grow. Whether it be fruits, trees, leaves, or shrubs—all of that power to make these things grow is contained within that rain. All of the ingredients—light, taste, and everything are within this rain that falls directly onto these trees and plants. There is a difference between the rainwater and the water that comes from the earth itself.

The water which comes from the earth comes out of these five elements—earth, fire, water, air, and ether. But with rainwater what happens is that it excludes the other four elements and gives the water alone. The water flows down the mountain. Combining that magnet with it that water then flows. Therefore, as soon as it falls, the rain water has great power in it; it brings with it the Power of God. This is the difference between the rainwater that comes from the clouds and the water that comes from the bottom of the earth.

This is the difference between a Prayer that has a connection with God and the prayer that has it connection with the earth, fire, water, air, ether, and with these things which we call 'spirituality'. These spiritual things do not possess that Power because all of the *saktis* and all of the forces and energies of the earth have sucked it up. All of that has been sucked up by the earth. It is only the sound that you can hear. That Magnet is lost. That Power which can make a thing grow is not contained within it.

The Treasure which can make your Soul and your Wisdom grow is contained in what comes from the heavens. What God wants is there. The thing that makes Compassion grow is there. The thing that makes Peacefulness and Tolerance grow is there. The thing that makes *Saboor* [Patience] grow is there. Contentment is there. Compassion is there, and also the thing that develops the quality of Equality to all lives exists there. The thing which develops the quality of cherishing and loving others' lives as your own exists there. That Power which allows all of these good intentions, Good Qualities, and Wisdom to grow is contained in that which comes from Him Himself. This comes as a Vibration from God.

A Guru who is an *Insān Kāmil* [a True Man]—if he is an *Insān Kāmil*—receives that Magnet from God. That is like the rain that falls. The rainwater has that Magnet within it. In the same way, that Power radiates from the words of the *Insān Kāmil*, and falls just as the rain does upon the herbs, weeds, and grass. As they accept this rain, they grow. Also your Faith, Determination, and Certitude will accept and absorb that Power from the *Kāmil Shaikh*. This *Imān* [Absolute Faith] will take it and absorb it. That Magnet will draw it. That Power will be drawn by that Magnet. It will pierce like this, with that sound of *errrrrrr*—and it will lift you up. Wherever you need to go, you can go. It will show how you can grow, how you can obtain bliss, and how you can make it exalted. It will show you how it can beautify you, and how your ailments can be cured.

It can cure your worst diseases and also show you how to prevent accidents. It will cure your cancer, your headaches, the distresses and diseases of your mind, your tiredness, your blood ties, your blood sugar, and other things. It will cure the diseases of the nerves, the defects of vision, and all of the dirt and bad odor that are within you. It will develop beauty in your faces, and your eyesight will become like that of a sixteen year old. Your hair will become very, very soft, and your mind will become very light. That Power will beautify the sound that comes from within you so that you can praise God. Your breath will be very light. That Power will cure torpor, the torpor of the bile. Your craziness will go away. It will change everything and make you Peaceful. It will develop you and exhibit you in Gods Own Beauty. It will show you the beauty of Compassion. It is a very, very great Power.

You have got to accept this and grow. If you grow like this, then through that Point you can achieve everything you need. Once you receive this Magnet, you will grow. Without this Magnet you try to learn by the mind, by the five elements, or by book knowledge, or by vibrations received from satan, and by performing satan's prayers. But these will do you no good. If you remain in the house of satan and pray, none of these sections will do you any good. We must rid ourselves of all of these things. You must try to receive that Magnetic Power of Wisdom, which has the power of developing you. Having received it, then you must do it as you now have been told. You have to think about it within your heart. There is no need for you to go on doing all of these things for the sake of God. For the sake of God, there is no reason for you to go on wasting your time shouting, "ha-hoo, hoo, hoo, ha."

God has given you two eyes in order to see. One is the sun. One is the moon. There are two nostrils. They are the *chandira kalai* [art of the moon] and the *sūriya kalai* [art of the sun]. One is for the world, the other is for *Gnānam* [Wisdom]. He has given you that tongue, the tongue to taste His Taste, and also the tongue that dances with greed and continuously ask for things. There are also two ears. One listens to God, and the other listens to the world. There are eight *qalbs* [hearts] which God has given you. The *Qalb* which is the Kingdom of God is the place from where God rules. The other seven taste hell and relish hell.

Like this, God has given us such things. He has given us two hands. The good things are done with the right hand and the evil things are done with the left hand. When you go to do a good thing, go with the right. The left belongs to evil. He has given you the right and the left feet. The right foot goes as *ill Allāhu*—except for Allah; the left goes as *Lā Illāha*—nothing exists. So when you walk, as you move the left foot say *Lā Illāha*, and as you move the right foot say *ill Allāhu*. The arms will also move left, right, left, right, resonating the same sound. Then the heart will vibrate in the same way, and the breath will also vibrate in the same way. When you proceed like this, the sight of the eyes will also operate in this manner. The breath will also radiate that. This can be compared to walking. For the right you put the right foot forward, and that is the section which communes with God. For the left you put the left foot forward, and that is the section of the body or illusion.

This is life. As we walk both of these must be done. The left, the body, belongs to the world. Whatever the body needs must be given to the body. What has to be given to your Soul, which is the right, has to be given to the Soul. The food for your Soul comes from God, and the food for the body comes from *māya* [illusion]. So, both duties have to be performed. We must walk in this way—left, right, left, right. For this you need not go and sit in one place. God has separated the two and given them to you. One is to perform the duties to the world, and the other is to perform the duties to God. He has given both of these. So you must conduct both of these sections in unity. If you can understand this, it will be very easy for you to carry on your daily life, and also it will be easy for you to reach God. Then receiving His Grace will be easy, and overcoming *māya* will also be easy. Then you can understand everything. You need to go in search of the Wisdom which can understand all of this.

In this state of understanding you need not waste even five seconds for the sake of God. He has Eyes all over, He has Ears all over. He is the One who can see everywhere. He is there intermingled in everything. He is the One who sees everything, both outside and inside. There is nothing that He does not see. There is no place that He is not seeing. He will give whatever each one needs or asks for.

There is a thing called outside and a thing called inside. In all of the games that we play there are two sections—either victory or loss. You are playing a game for two things—either to win or to lose. One is a losing game, and one is a winning game. In life it is also like this. This is the game of the body.

Yet, my children, by reflecting on Him, thinking of Him, depending on Him, being aware of Him from inside, and by compressing His Love within, you must ascertain His Qualities from within. His Justice must be firm within your hearts. His Trust must be firm within you. His Patience must be firm within you. You must have *Tawakkal* or Absolute Trust in Him. Keep His 3,000 Gracious Qualities and His Actions within you. If you can store these Qualities within you, and if as you walk your intention is: *Lā Ilāha*—there is nothing other than you, O God; and *ill Allāhu*—You are God—then you will have that as the intention within your heart. That intention will operate within you. In each one of your actions the proof of it will be exhibited to you. Even as you breathe in and out this will be operating and working. As if you are pumping, it will go on operating. So as you are going it is there. That will also go on operating and working as you walk. It is not where it was; it is going on. It is operating, continuously going on. Your intention is also going on circulating around. As you go on walking this intention is also circulating around. When both operate together, that is That. That is Prayer. That is That State. As That grows in you, your mind and that dog [desire] will not stay there. Only His Wonders, His Beauty, His Light, and His Taste will develop.

Without your knowing it, as you go with this intention, His Honey will come to you. His Milk will come to you. Without your knowing it, His Taste will come to you. It will come without your body even realizing it. It will come into you as a Vibration. That is the One Thing that can overcome your death. The left will not be aware of it, but the right will be receiving it. When you are doing this and receiving this, the left will not be aware of it. When you look at this, both the left and the right look alike.

Your ailments, diseases, disasters, distresses, griefs, sorrows, and such things are not the fault of God. Children, gems within my eyes, our driving is incorrect. The license that we have been given is correct, but we drive incorrectly. We have no experience at driving this vehicle, this body. We have been shown everything. Where the left foot should go automatically, it does not go. Where the arm should go, it does not go. You must know automatically how your foot should operate the accelerator and the brakes. You must switch on the lights. The hand has to operate the gear and the steering wheel automatically. It must work automatically in this way. The One who gave the license is correct. The One who taught you driving is also correct. But we have forgotten it. We have forgotten this driving. We just took hold of the steering wheel and forgot the technique for driving. So what can we do? We are just driving. We are driving our vehicle on a road where there are many accidents. Wherever you look there are accidents. We have given up this automatic work, and we have abandoned the awareness of how these things should work automatically. We have abandoned the awareness of where each hand should go, where each arm should go, where each leg should go, and where each foot should go.

Now what are we doing? When we are confronted with an accident, we have to look to see where to put the foot. We put the wrong foot down, and by the time we discover it, we have already met with an accident. First we must look ahead, then we must proceed carefully. These sections should go in advance. The other sections should be automatically working. The section of the hand has to operate automatically as it should. The section of the feet has to operate as it should operate. The eyes must work as they should. Wisdom should do its work automatically. Awareness should do what it has to do. Like this, if everything is correctly operating, there will be no accidents. We have forgotten this technique. Having forgotten this technique, we are learning new methods of steering, new ways of driving, and new techniques. This is why we meet with accidents. That is why these dangers are confronting us. Some have lost their eyes, some have lost their noses. Some have broken their backs. In others, joints have become dislocated, and some have twisted their necks. This is because our driving is incorrect. The license is correct, but the way we practice is wrong. This is the fault. You are acquiring new methods of driving, but they are causing accidents.

Therefore, my dear children, gems of my eyes, you must think. Decide what is needed for each section and each circumstance, and proceed with that very carefully. Using your Wisdom proceed like that. Using your awareness proceed very carefully. Like that, for each and every point discriminate carefully, know what is needed, and then proceed. If you proceed in this way, then the Treasure that God has given us to prevent accidents will prevent all of these accidents. No accidents will ever occur. No danger will occur. We are careless. Each thing is not operating where it should operate. If each section were working in the section where it should work, then accidents would never occur.

Therefore, children, gems of my eye, each method that our Father has given us, each quality that He has given us, each experience that He has given us, must be taken in with feeling, awareness, intellect, judgment, Wisdom, Divine Analytic Wisdom, and Divine Luminous Wisdom. Through feeling came awareness; through awareness came intellect; through intellect came judgment; through that came Wisdom; through Wisdom came Divine Analytic Wisdom; and through that came the *Perr-Arivu* or Divine Luminous Wisdom. Through that comes Plenitude; through that Plenitude comes Overpowering Effulgence; through that Overpowering Effulgence comes Completeness, the Entire Overpowering Effulgence of that Power. The Power that comes out of that is God. He is the One that is intermingled in every life. We must think about this. We must try to reach this State.

We need to understand what thing is needed for each circumstance. If we can know that correctly, then we can prevent every accident that might occur. No accident will ever come to us. We will never meet with any accident. We have ruined ourselves. That is what has happened. We are causing these accidents to come to us. That is the reason these accidents occur. You must think about this.

Dear children, we must understand how our life is to be conducted. There is the earth wire, there is the Light wire; both of these must be in unity. One belongs to God, the other belongs to the body. The section of the earth is the section which relates to the five elements and *māya*. No matter how high you put the Light, the earth wire must come back to the earth. Even if you take this wire up to the clouds, the earth wire has got to be in the earth. This body has an earthly connection. For that it needs the earth. Its energy and its work have to be connected to the earth. It needs the earth. However, when you connect that Light to the heavens, that is the connection to God. When you light your Soul with God, then that Vibration, that Light, comes from the Father alone. That is there, and this is down on the earth; both are needed. This is needed, the other is also needed.

You must know how to analyze and separate the two. Perform the duty to your body, and perform the duty to God. You need both. If you can organize these two sections correctly, both of these can be protected. Before your time of judgment is over you must understand this. For That the food must come from there, and for this the food must come from the earth. The charge for the Soul should come from there, from God. It is from there that you receive the charge. The charge for the elements—earth, fire, air, water, and space—has to be obtained from the earth itself. The elements of the body, need water and food. Everything that will charge up the body must come from the earth. For the Soul the charge must come from the heavens; it must come from there. The charge for that battery of your Soul has to come from God. The charge for your body has got to come from the elements and the earth.

If you can understand this with your Wisdom, if you can understand this State, if you fix the wires correctly, and if you plug each line into the correct socket, then you will know what it is. Put the correct number into the correct line. Now you are not communicating with *that* plug or with that Point. You are not communicating on *that* telephone. You do not know which number to plug into. You do not know which number to call. So how can you converse? There are telephones from house to house, and there are numbers for each of them, but you must have the correct number if you want to call. The telephone numbers are given in the books, so get the correct code number and then dial. Only then will it ring there. Then you can converse. Without knowing the code and the correct number, if you use a different code and different numbers, then it will ring in a different place. You will get the wrong numbers. You take different codes and you call, but you will not get the reply that you want if you dial these wrong numbers. You cannot communicate with these numbers. You must learn from the department that will teach you the correct code and the correct number. You must attempt to study that. If you can find those codes and numbers, and if you have got that telephone book before you, then you will know that this code and this number will take you to God. This number and this code will take you to Jesus. This code and this number will take you to Moses. This one will take you to Muhammad, this one to Jacob, this one to Michael. With this number you can dial for Joseph, on this number you can get to Johah. So, you must first get the correct code and number, and then dial. You must note each code and each number. Then you can ring them up and talk. You must know that. If you can learn that code, it is easy to speak to them. It is very easy then.

What you are doing now is ringing without knowing the

number and the code. You go on ringing and ringing—*yoga* ringing—you are even standing on your head and ringing. You are keeping your legs up and your head down and ringing. You recite *ahh-ing* and *ring*. None of these codes will work. All of these numbers relate to the earth. They will only ring the earth. The numbers that you are ringing are not of the right section. This is a completely different section. So what do you need? You need the right number. If you want the right number you must get it from the right side. If you want the earth number, you will have to go to the left side or to the earth.

Let us think of this a little and act accordingly. Learn the True Numbers. This is not a thing that you can be taught for money; you need not spend money for this. You can learn it for free. There is no need to pay a hundred and fifty dollars to learn to recite *ahh*, *ing*, *oom*. There may be people who like to do this sort of thing. But, children, you must go in search of Wisdom and then search for that Point within Wisdom. That is good. Then you can obtain it easily. Communing will be easy. Seeing will be easy. There are so many wonders there, so much happiness and bliss there.

My children, gems within my eye, please search for and obtain this. Do it the way that you have now been told. Reflect on what you heard just now. Try to obtain this Magnetic Power from the Guru, as the grass and herbs obtain it. You must be very careful. This is a very sharp Point. You cannot see it with your eyes. You have to draw it in through the Magnet of your Wisdom, and through your Faith, Determination, and Certitude. These things must be kept within. Then these codes and numbers can be learned. That is easy. Take these numbers correctly. Please think of this, then it will be very good.

The Camera

Children, gems of my eye, within us there is a camera that films everything. How is that? Those reels are our desires. The mind is the camera. There is a mind within a mind, which is the world. There is another section within that which is the ocean of *māya* [illusion]. There are many things to investigate within this ocean. There is also another ocean, the ocean of desire. Within that is another ocean, the ocean of sex. Within that there is another ocean, the ocean of torpor. Like this, there are many other aspects. These aspects are within the same section.

Intellect investigates this. Intellect is the director. He is the director of the film, directing that camera which is in the heart. Intellect investigates this and displays it as science. Science can show an atom as a huge mountain. Science has also brought down the might of a mountain to that of an atom. It can make the sky appear closer to you. What is near can be focused and shown as if it were in the sky. A small image can be magnified to a huge image and shown to you. A big image can be shown to you as a tiny dot. Like this, there are many things that science has done. What exists as a very tiny thing within the ocean can be shown as a huge thing. The huge thing can be minimized and shown as a small point. A big fire can be made to appear even bigger. Through certain tricks with the camera the same fire can be shown as a small fire. Like this, through intellect the mind focuses these things and shows them. We look at this. Dolls are made to sing, dance, and talk. You can see all these things.

Man has this camera within him. This camera films the section of *māya*. The intellect magnifies the sun, moon, and stars and makes them appear as huge things. Huge things are shown as a tiny dot. That is how this camera of the mind works. It can make a big ocean appear to be a tiny atom. It can make a tiny atom appear to be something huge. Those are the tricks of the camera. Like this, it films millions and millions of pictures. Your mind has the capacity to take these pictures. The director of all this is the intellect. Desire is the reels, and *māya* is the camera. The mind is the darkness. It is through this darkness that everything is filmed. Like this, it is filming us and exhibiting it to us. Having seen this, we give it great praise or blame. These are all the tricks of the camera which put out the fire of Truth and exhibit the fire of falsehood. It overturns houses and causes oceans to overflow. These are the tricks of the intellect, the director. These are the tricks of the elements. These are the tricks of the senses. These are the tricks of the earth, tricks of fire, tricks of water, tricks of air, tricks of the colors and vapors. And these are the tricks of the mind.

Through these tricks the camera takes pictures. It magnifies a small thing as a big ocean or as a huge world. It makes a small thing appear as a great pleasure or as a big heaven. Like this, the mind films these things and shows them. You look at the film and say, "*Ah, ah, ah!*" experiencing pleasure. These are really the tricks of the mind, tricks of the intellect, tricks of the senses, tricks of desire, and tricks of illusion. Through these we see big things made small and small things made big. We look at this and say, "These are great wonders."

In truth, you really have to become the director. But you need Wisdom in order to do this. That One called Wisdom has to come. Wisdom must become the Superintendent of this director. If this is the way it operates, and if He holds the camera He will set it correctly. No matter how much you have magnified it, He will check it with His Wisdom. If He checks all the *māya* that was shown, He knows that if He takes an atom and cuts it into millions, billions, or even trillions of pieces and takes one of those pieces, that small piece will be equal to this whole world of *māya*. Then also He knows all the tricks that were shown. You need to know how to set this camera. You need the Commander to check this camera and to set it properly.

This is not a great thing. The camera just exhibited to you whatever it wanted. These are the tricks of the camera—tricks of the mind, tricks of desire, tricks of illusion, tricks of the intellect, tricks of the five elements, tricks of the five senses, and tricks of the darkness of satan. That is what we see now. We have to check with Wisdom. If you analyze this section and see, you will know that this world is a very tiny thing.

You saw many wonders. But in reality there were no fires, there were no volcanoes, there was no destruction, there were no gales, there were no floods, there were no situations in which one was victorious and the other one was killed. If you check properly and see, then you will find out that in reality God is the One who always existed. His Power cannot be shaken at all. The rest are all tricks of the intellect, tricks of the director, tricks of desire, tricks of the monkey mind, tricks of *maya*, tricks of satan, and tricks of the elements. That is what was shown to you.

Reflect on this, develop Wisdom, see and analyze through this, and set this camera properly. Then realize *awwal*, *dunyaa*, and *ākhir* [the beginning, the present world, and the hereafter]. If you focus on these three worlds with that Wisdom, the world will be as I said before—one trillion, trillion, trillionth part of what you have been shown. This is of no value. This is a very, very small thing. It is only through this mind, these elements, and through these tricks that you see this world as a big and mighty thing. It is really only a very, very tiny dot in the universe.

When you transcend this and see above, you will realize that there is a mighty Power there. (This place is not even visible then.) God is the One who can swallow this camera and everything else. He is All-Pervasive.

This place, which we now see magnified and full of wonders through the tricks of the camera, is not even a visible dot for that Power. The *sifāt* [creation] is a small thing. This world exists as a secret to Him. This is a tiny thing. Does a thing like this world exist for Him? It is a thing that He does not even think about. Even when He looks, He cannot see it. To God this tiny thing is a secret. To us God is a Secret and the world is magnified and made to appear big. Because of these tricks of the camera, we do not see Him, but we make this world into a big wonder.

If we can discover this Wisdom and focus and set this camera properly, we will see *'ālam* and *arwāh*, the universe and the world of souls. We will see everything—*awwal*, *dunyaa*, and *ākhir*.

If you set this camera with Wisdom and analyze section by section, you will then realize that everything you saw before was just the tricks of this camera. The tricks magnified these things and showed them to you. You will realize that they were tricks of the monkey mind, tricks of desire, tricks of satan, tricks of *māya*, tricks of the elements. That is what was magnified and shown to you.

In reality, if you see, none of these things exist. If you set the camera correctly and see, you will know that there is only that One Power of God which contains everything. Therefore, if you can set the heart correctly and focus it with Wisdom beyond the point where intellect focused, you will know the subtlety of each and everything. Then those tricks of the camera will have gone. Then you will realize how all that you saw was false. Only if you set it correctly will you know that there is only One God. You will see the Light, the Son of God. You will see the *Zāt*, the Essence of God, and you will see the Grace of God. Everything else will exist as a particle within a particle. If you search with your Wisdom and focus it correctly, you will know that what you see now are the tricks of the mind. This is what the mind has researched. But if you set it correctly and focus it on God, everything will come right.

If you do not set it correctly, all the pictures that are shown will be the tricks of the mind, the tricks of the camera, the tricks of intellect, the tricks of desire, the tricks of birth, and the tricks of the five elements. This is what we see.

Therefore, reflect on this and understand this. If you act accordingly, it will be very good. If you understand this, you can say good-bye to the world, you can say good-bye to the tricksters. It is like that.

The Flower Garden

Children, the gems of my eyes, my loving children, the gems of my eyes who are seeking the Love and Teachings of our Eternal Father, may He bestow His Love on you. May He grant you what you are searching for.

Children, gems of my eyes, our Father has given everything to us. He has given everything to us. He has also given us a 'television' or a power by which we can understand all that He has bestowed upon us. He has created the world, and He has also created His story. He has created the actors for His story and also the people who are going to see this acting. He has also given the television through which these actors can be seen. He has given you wisdom and awareness so that you will be able to see the praise-worthiness and the faults in the actors. He has given a mirror in order for us to see this. He has given us everything.

Dear children, gems of my eyes, this section of creation can be compared to a big farm. There are many kinds of farms. We are the farmers. There is a cow farm, a cattle farm, a horse farm, a goat farm, a sheep farm, a poultry farm, a flower farm, an apple farm, and a grape farm. Like that, there are many different kinds of farms, so that, whatever each person needs to cultivate at each period of time, he may cultivate and develop it. If one wants or desires something, he can produce it. If you need wheat, rice, rye, corn, peanuts, or whatever you need, it can be planted and grown in this large farm of the world. This is creation. Each thing that is needed can be cultivated. What is needed for each one can be cultivated and developed. We look at these things and say, "How beautiful this apple orchard is. How beautiful this grape arbor is. How beautiful these pears are. How beautiful these plums are. How beautiful these nuts and almonds are." Like this many things are said. These are all things that can be cultivated in this farm. Many things are cultivated, such as cabbage, beets, and potatoes. Some say that these things are very tasty, and they eat them. Praising, finding fault, bitterness, sourness, sweetness—all of these things exist in this farm.

In the same way, within this farm of the mind you can experience many things, such as happiness and sorrow. Many emotions are experienced in this farm. But, dear children, please think. This is the section of creation which contains earth, fire, water, air, and ether (the colors, the sun, the moon, and the stars). We can see these. All of these things belong to this farm. The sky is one section of this farm; the earth is another section of this farm. Each one has a farm within it. So whatever you need to do in order to cultivate your farm, do it, and that will bear fruit. Whatever you need to do, do it, and your farm will bear fruit. It will bear fruit. It is like this in this creation formed out of the five elements: earth, fire, water, air, and ether.

Similarly, in this spiritual farm, this is how it grows. There are vapors and spirits. There is fire. There are the angels Gabriel, Michael, *Isrāfīl*, and *Izrā'eel* (the angel of death). There are also the elements and demons. All of these belong to that section of creation which is 'spiritual'. These things grow in the farm of the mind. Those things that are called spiritual also relate to the vapors. There may be many kinds of spiritual things, but all of these relate to that farm. These spiritual things grow in that farm of the mind. In the same way that things are planted in this world, things can also be planted in your mind, in your intentions, and in your memories. Certain things can be planted, such as methods of prayer, methods of spirituality, methods of intending, and your intentions. You can grow these in that farm of the mind. In each of these farms, whatever you organize and plant will grow. What grows here in the mind is called spiritual. Those things which grow in the farm of the mind are the things that are called spiritual. What is grown outside in this earth is also called a farm. You call this the apple farm, flower farm, and various other kinds of farms. Like that, in the section of the mind there is also a farm.

The farm of the mind is the opposite of the earth farm. These earth farms can be seen, but the mind farms appear as shadows. The farm that you grow outside can be seen. Mind and desire look at these things and say, 'good' or 'bad'. The inner farm that develops is the spiritual farm. There are four hundred trillion, ten thousand such farms. It is like this. Within the senses there is a farm where bulls and cattle exist. There is also a jungle farm where you have tigers and leopards. There is a snake farm, there is a chicken or poultry farm. There is also a farm of goats which bite and nibble at everything. There are farms for cows and donkeys, farms for horses and ponies. All of these animals are found in this farm of the mind.

In the same way, the earth farm is also developing. Now these things that you see in this earth farm are in a form. But the mind farm exists in a formless state; it exists only as a shadow form. Here, in the earth, this farm exists in a form; but there, in the mind, it exists in a formless state or as a shadow.

Yet, my brother, my children, you need that 'television' which was mentioned earlier in order to understand this. You need that mirror in order to see this. The spiritual farm and the worldly farm are both farms. According to the seasons, whatever you plant in these farms will grow. If you want miracles, they will grow. If you want magic tricks, they will grow. If you want satan, that will grow. You can grow these things. Whatever you want can be grown. If you want the horse of the mind, that will grow. If you want milk, that will grow. If you want a goat which will butt everything, that will also grow. You can grow all of these things. Inside, you are growing everything in the form of a shadow, and outside, it is being grown in a form. Both can be cultivated and grown. One is inside and one is outside.

There is a certain time or season for this. There is a season when apples grow and ripen. Now that season is over and everything has been picked. Now the picking season is finished, and the fruits are brought to the supermarket to be sold. Now the apple trees are bare. The pear trees, cherry trees, and grape vines are all bare. That taste is not found there now, and that happiness is not there now. Whatever you grew in your farms has been picked now. You have picked the crops and everything is finished. At one time you were very happy to see the fruits; and when you tasted them, some were sour and some were sweet. The fruits existed in many ways. It is like that. Some fruits are very sweet and some fruits are sour, yet all of these fruits exist within the same farm.

Now all the flowers are fading away. With the change of the seasons, whatever we planted went away. The other farms are also the same. These miracles, these prayers, the *mantras*, the magics, the meditations, the *yoga*, the *sariyai*, *kiriyai, yogam* [three of the spiritual steps], and all of these spiritual things that you do are like those trees which became bare. In the same way that the trees became bare, these shadows will also become bare. One is a form, and the other is only a shadow. It is the shadow of these things that is found in the mind. Outside, you find these things existing in form.

What the mind accepts as good, bad, happiness, smiling, laughing, or praiseworthy is this same farm. You need to think about this, my children. The same farm that you are cultivating within, you are also cultivating without. These are the actors, these are the acts. This is what you must see on that television. This is what you have to understand through that mirror of Wisdom. This is the world, these are the acts of the world and these are the farms. It is this farm that the body is cultivating. The mind cultivates it, desire cultivates it, the earth cultivates it. The angels all cultivate it: *Adam*, earth, cultivates it. *Michael*, water, cultivates it. *Gabriel*, the lights, the intellect; *Isrāfil*, the 2,128 different kinds of vapors; *Yemen*, the angel of death and fire—all of these cultivate and grow this farm. All of them do this. The mind, desire, illusion, and satan all get together and cultivate these farms. These are the farms that are found outside and inside.

Man tastes the happiness and sorrows that he grows within these farms. He tastes the fruits from both of these farms. But finally, all of these are picked and taken to the supermarket. Where do they all go? They will all finally go to the supermarket. The apples will go to the supermarket. These things cannot be kept here for a long time; so finally, they will be picked and taken to the supermarket. It is like this. All of our prayers, all the spirituality, and all that we grow in this farm of the mind finally goes to the supermarket of *māya* [illusion]. All that is cultivated and grown within the mind has to go to that same supermarket. It has to go to that market of satan. Just as what grows outside on the earth goes to this supermarket, what grows inside goes to the supermarket of illusions. Both trees will become bare once the season changes. Once the season changes, both will become bare. This is how the life of this body is. One is inside, the other is outside. The business that both farms do is the same farming.

The television of Truth has been placed within your heart. In order that you may see the act, God has also given you a good mirror in which to see and understand it. He has given you Wisdom in order that you may see through that mirror and in order to make it clear. He has given you that pure, clear water of *Īmān* [Absolute, Complete Faith, Certitude, and Determination] to clean the mirror and make it clear. God has said, "Clean it with this." In order that you may clean the mirror with conviction, firmness, and great strength, He has given you Faith, Certitude, and Determination. He has given you Faith, Certitude, and Determination to rub hard and remove all of that dirt. He has given you *Ilm*, or the Ocean of Knowledge, to discard that dirt. He has given you the Plenitude of His Grace so that you will remove that dirt, discard that which is wrong, and make that mirror clear. All of this is within you.

You have to understand these farms. Everyone has to understand these farms of creation. You also have to understand the farms of your prayers and spirituality. In order to know and understand this, you need the *Ilm of Arivu*, which is the Ocean of Knowledge of Wisdom. You must try to search for this. And in this state, you must develop another farm—not the farm that was created by your mind, not the farm that was created by your body. These were created with selfishness. These are for yourself, for your body, and for illusions. The farm of the mind is for the five elements and for the food of illusion. It is for the *kalais* or the 64 arts and sciences. The farm of the body is one kind of farm, the farm of the mind is a different farm. The third farm is yet another kind of farm. So each one's individual farm has to be cultivated within. Whatever one cultivates and grows will bear fruit.

Therefore, my dear children, think of this. You must think of this. You must think of these farms. These farms are all related to systems. They grow and disappear during various seasons. What the trees do is also according to the seasons. What the mind does is also according to the seasons. They all change. What the earth does is also a system, it goes according to the seasons. What vapor does is also the same. What water does is also according to a system and a season. Ether and *māya* also go according to a system and a season. All of these change with the seasons. They all have a beginning and an end. They bear fruit and become bare again. They flower, and then the flowers fade away and drop off. These are not permanent. There is the period of winter when there is snow. Then there is a season of plowing and a season of planting. A thing grows, then it disappears and becomes bare. In this way it goes on changing seasonally. This is the way of these plowing and farming seasons. You start it, you cultivate it, and then it ends. There is the season when it is bare and also the season when it bears fruit.

It is the same for this farm of the body and for the farm of the mind. What you cultivate from within is called the spiritual farm. What you cultivate from outside is the material farm. Who are the actors that praise, blame, and find fault? Mind and desire do this.

My dear children, you must think of this. Both are farms. The spiritual farm is what the mind does. It is in a shadow form. What is outside is what your body and the elements perform. These are farms with form. The other is a shadow farm. Both are being done. You must think and reflect about this.

It is necessary that you cultivate a farm. *That* farm is the Farm of God. If you grow *that* Apple Tree, it will always bear fruit. There is no season or system for it. If you grow *that* Flower, it will be a Flower forever. If you grow it according to the correct methods, then it has no seasons. It does not need earth, fire, water, or air. It does not need the elements. It does not have seasonal changes. It is a Natural Farm. The apples, grapes, or whatever you cultivate and grow in that Farm will never diminish. It will never be destroyed. That Taste will never change. That Beauty will never change. It exists as the One Point which is naturally permanent. That is a Farm which is more subtle than an atom. It is more subtle than a particle of a particle of a particle of a particle of an atom. That Farm commences from His Beauty, His Qualities, His Actions, His Sight, His Intentions, His Thoughts, His Completeness, His Power, His Grace, and His Light. That Farm has to grow in these Qualities.

That is *Īmān* and that is the *Kalimah*. That is the *Alif*, the letter *Alif* [ا]. That One, that *Alif*, is He. You have to plant that Seed. That Seed is the Truth. That is pure, pure, pure Gold. That is like Pure Gold. You must plant that Seed in that Pure Place. That is the Seed of *Firdaus* [the eighth complete heaven]. When the seedling comes out, that is *Firdaus,* that is Paradise. That One Tree is called *Sidratul-*

muntahā. (In Tamil it is called *Katpahavarichan.*) It will have
Flowers, Fruits, Light, Grace, Wisdom, Honey, and Milk.
Whatever you need, you can take from that Tree. There is no
time, there is no season. You can take from the Tree of
Sidratul-muntahā whatever you need at that time. The Form
of that Tree is God. It is like a flower garden. It is the Tree of
Love. It is the Tree of *Īmān.* It is the Tree of the Effulgence of
Wisdom. It is the Completeness of *Noor,* the Resplendence of
God. It is the Power of God. You can take and eat whatever
you need from that Tree. It is One Point, One Seed. It is the
One Pure Farm. It is the Farm of Light which has no earth,
fire, water, air, or ether in it. It grows through the Power of
God alone. It will grow only in the place of Complete Purity.
If you plant that Seed with strong and perfect determination,
then it will grow with many branches. The branches from one
Seed of the *Sidratul-muntahā* Tree can cover all the
universes. The *Sidratul-muntahā* has within it whatever you
need. It is without seasons, it never diminishes, and it is
never ending. In each fruit there are 70,000 different tastes.
In each flower there are 70,000 different kinds of fragrances.
Within each drop there are 70,000 tastes of honey.

Like that, when you dissect it section by section and
look, everything is within it. Whatever you want can be
tasted in it. There are no cows there, but there is milk. There
is fruit, but no tree. There is taste, but no form. There is
milk, but the color of white is not there. There is honey, but it
is not a honey that can be seen. All of the fruits are there, yet
it does not contain the color or the form. That section is not
there. Whatever you need, the taste of that is given. There is
no house or palace, but there is a Palace where you can stay.
There is no male and female, but there is the Taste. There
are no bathrooms or toilets there, but everything is burned
away. His Love, His Mystery, His *Qudrat* [Power], His

Benevolence, His Beauty, and His Bliss exist there. There is no train or bus service. There are no trains, planes, or buses, but you can travel. There is no money, but that Taste of Completeness is there. That Fullness is there. There is no change of season. There is no birth and there is no death. That is the One which has none of these.

That Seed is the Seed of *Alif*. It is the Seed of God. You have to plant that Seed in Purity. You have to cultivate and nurture that Seed. That is the correct prayer. If that grows, then *you* do not exist. If you can plant that Seed firmly within you, then when that Seed grows, the elements that are covering it will be destroyed. The elements there will be killed by the Seed as it grows. As soon as it grows, it will kill or destroy anything that is beneath it. Only the root will go deep within. The form of it will be burned off; and when that form goes, this Seed will grow. That form will be consumed and this Seed will grow. Therefore, when you plant this Seed in that Place of Purity, this Seed will consume all that was covering the Purity. It will destroy desire. All of these will be burned off and only that Tree will grow.

When that which covers the Purity is destroyed, then the 'I' does not exist. There is no mind, there is no body, there is no fire, and there is no world. There is nothing. All of these energies have been completely consumed. Only that One alone will remain. That is: *Lā Ilāha*—There is nothing other than You, O God; *ill Allāhu*—You alone are God. Wherever you plant this Seed, as soon as it grows, it will destroy everything else. As soon as it is planted within the Pure Heart, it will destroy everything else. All of these farms which had been covering it, the farm outside and the farm inside, will be consumed by that Purity. Both of these farms will be consumed by that Purity. They will be consumed and destroyed. Then I do not exist, there is no 'I' at all then.

Other than You, O God, nothing exists. All of the *mantras* are gone. Time, space, spiritual devotion, farms, and everything have been destroyed. You are the Only One. That is the *Sidratul-muntahā*.

That One Tree is the One which spreads all over the universes. The branches of that One Tree will spread all over the 18,000 universes. It will be your flower garden, it will be your fruit orchard, it will be your apple orchard. Fruits, raisins, and all things are there. This is the Thing that you have to nurture. This is the One that has transcended time, space, and seasons. These spiritual farms, shadow farms, and form farms will all be destroyed.

That One Seed, that One Thing, that One Farm is the One that will give you whatever you want. That is the One Tree. That is the One which has no season, no time, and no space. There is no season for flowers, for fruits, or for picking. That is the Eternal Natural Farm. We must cultivate that Farm. That Farm is Pure. That Farm is Complete Purity. That is the One which has to be cultivated. If you cultivate only That, my children, then That is the Only Good. If you can develop That, then you will be My Children. You will be My Children of Good Qualities. Then That will be your Father. We can see and reach our Father then. He has a beautiful Taste. Please ask with these Good Intentions and these Good Qualities.

If this is not done, then that farm which you are cultivating and growing outside and the spiritual farm which you are cultivating inside will both be the same. The section of *maya* and the section of satan are both farms. You praise these or you find fault. This is not good. This leads you to death, this is death. There is a beginning and there is an end for this. This is of no use. You have to think and reflect on this.

Last night someone invited me to a house. I do not know what country it was. I went to Colombo and we attended to some matters there. And then we went to another place to attend to some other matters. After that, I was invited to another house. They had been inviting me there for many years, so I said, "Right! We shall go there." It was a beautiful home, a very, very beautiful home. As I was going inside I saw a section of the house. It was a very big house. They had spread a velvet carpet on the floor. The velvet carpet was spread along the center of the floor. The carpet was of many colors. They called and invited me there with a great deal of respect. There were beautiful flowers on each side of the carpet. On each side of the velvet carpet there were beautiful, beautiful flower trees, all blossoming beautifully. There were flower trees inside the house. When I looked at it, those flowers and the carpet were very, very beautiful. There were many beautiful flowers with very beautiful and subtle colors.

They called me respectfully, and we went in. There was a place for us to sit. Everything was organized. As we were going in, we smelled the sweetness of the fragrance of the flowers. I told the child, "Oh, you have been calling for a long time. You have cultivated and grown these flowers very beautifully. These flowers that are inside the house are also very beautiful."

Then she said, "It is to invite my Father that I have done all of this."

"Ah," I said, "did you cultivate all of this?" There were also many fruits there for us. Then I said, "Yes, all of these things that you have cultivated here and all that you have offered to us are very, very beautiful. But to me it is like a bad smell." Then I said, "Give some of the fruits to the children."

They brought the fruits to the children, and then she said, "My Father, won't you take one?"

"For me it is not needed," I said, "but you share this with the children."

When they were finished I spoke a few words: "It is all right that you invited me here, and this garden is very beautiful to look at. But come here. Now see this."

Where we went, there were flowers one day old, two days old, three days old, four days old, and five days old. This is the way they were blooming. There were flowers there up to six days old. They were blooming beautifully.

Then I told the child, "I have come to your house. All of the flowers are very beautiful. As I was coming inside, they were also beautiful. You invited me here beautifully, and the flowers were also beautiful. But now, when I look at it—now just see."

By this time they had all faded and fallen. The flowers that were one day old had decayed and decomposed, and they were all smelling foul. Those that were six days old were decaying and smelling foul. All of them were spoiled. The foul smell was indescribable.

I called the child and said, "Come here. It is this that you have grown all this time. This is one day old, this is two days old, this is three days old, this is four days old, this is five days old, and this is six days old. This is what you have grown. You grew these so beautifully, and for a long time you had the intention of inviting me; but what is the use of this. Now I cannot go back there, it smells so foul. For this occasion, you picked a seed, you planted it well, you watered it, and you fertilized it. Day and night you looked after it. You did all of this. Yesterday it was flowering and today it has faded. In one day it is finished. When I came here they were beautiful, but a few minutes afterwards they started to fade and decay. What is the use of your taking all this trouble to grow these flowers? You have not grown that Natural Flower, that Flower which will be Eternal. This thing that you grew with so much difficulty smells foul now. See, I cannot go back there, it smells so bad. So now, please see and reflect upon what Seed *could* be grown within this house which will be Eternal and which will never die. Think of that and try to grow that Seed. That will be good."

I do not know which child it was, but one of the children took my hand and we came out. I said to her, "Do not keep these things and invite me. If you keep these decorations and invite me, this is how it will be; these things will fade away. My child, try to cultivate that Good Thing. Plant that Eternal Seed." And then I came back.

This is how people try to invite God. With the pleasures of the eyes and the pleasures of the mind they make a flower garden of the world. And keeping all of these spiritual demons, they decorate them and invite God. They invite God. These are all things which will die off in one day, in two days, or three; and by the sixth day they are completely decomposed.

These five things—lust, anger, hastiness, falsehood, and greed—look very beautiful, and they are colorful. But before you go inside and come out, everything has decayed and smells bad. This is what they had decorated the house with. This is the garden of that house. Although she had beautified it very much, it was decorated with these five things and with the arts, with illusions, with the sixty-four sexual arts, with earth, fire, water, air, ether, and with mind and desire. She had decorated that house using these things. This is the kind of flower garden that had been cultivated and grown there. When you looked the appearance was very beautiful. But before you could enter and return, everything had decayed.

It is like this. You decorate this house with the elements, and you invite God there. But nothing exists there, everything fades and dies. Everything smells foul. You should not build this house like that. You cannot cultivate this flower garden like that. This House of God cannot be developed like that. It is not these decorations, it is His Decorations that you need. His Flower of Love is needed, His Compassion is needed, His Qualities are needed. It is through His Beauty that you must decorate. His House has to be decorated in this way. His Duty has to decorate this House. His Sight, His Intentions, His Memory, and His Thoughts should be complete within His House. That Heaven, that *Firdaus*, has to be decorated in this manner. If you decorate with that Point and then invite God, only then will He come. That will be Eternal, that will not have an end. There will be no trees, but there will be flowers. There will be no fruits, but there will be taste. There is no cow, but still there is milk. There are no cattle, but the farm exists. There is no honey, but honey exists. There is no house, but Heaven exists. There are no planes or trains, but there is travelling. There is nothing, but God exists.

Like that, this is the Beauty that you have to cultivate and grow. It is such a thing that you have to cultivate. This is the House of our Father. Our Father is in that Place. You must try to search for this Point. If you do not do this, all else will be of no use. Whatever you have decorated and kept in that flower garden is no good. Although you have decorated it with so much, that house is no good. The Father cannot reside there. It will smell foul to Him. That house appeared beautiful, but before you could enter it and return, the flowers had all decayed and died.

My dear children, what is it that is needed? There are these two different kinds of farms. One has form and the other develops in a formless manner. What should you be aware of? You should be aware of that Natural Farm. That is Purity. That is the Purity of the Heart. That is the Flower Garden. There is an Eternal Flower there and that is the House of our Father. That is where He resides. What Flower should be grown there? What Seed should be grown there? What Seed should be planted there? That Seed is the Truth. You have to plant that, and you have to cultivate that. Truly, this is what you must do.

This is Prayer. If this grows, everything else will be consumed. The mind will be destroyed. Desire will be destroyed. Birth will be destroyed. Earth, fire, water, air, ether—all of the elements will die. That One alone will exist. So, what should you plant? Please plant that Seed. Please try to develop that Flower Garden. Try to do what I have just told you. You need to cultivate this. This is the Truth. You must try to fulfill this. Each one of you must do this. This is the duty we have to perform. For this you need the Wisdom to know how to cultivate that Farm. You need Patience. You need Faith, Certitude, and Determination—*Īmān*. You need *Īmān*. And you must try to develop that 'television' or mirror through which you can see these. Then you can see this and understand it. Then it is easy. Do you understand? My daughters and sons, do you understand this? This is the way of the Father's Farm.

Ameen.

My love you, my children.

The Prophets

At the time when the earth showed pride, God controlled the force of the earth through the agencies of water, air, fire, and mountains. Then He implanted the Power of His *Saboor*—His Patience—and subdued the qualities of the earth with it. When the water showed pride, He subdued it by the use of the mountains, the winds, the height of the mountains, the valleys, the air, the earth, and by filth, worms, and insects. He subdued the water by the *Da'wat*—the Wealth of His Truth—and by *Saboor*. When the fire showed pride, He subdued it through the agencies of water and air, through the Gaze of His *Qudrat*—His Power—and through His Patience. When the air showed pride, He controlled it by the use of huge mountains, by the earth, and by the Gaze of His *Qudrat*. When the ether showed pride, He controlled it by the use of seven things, and by the clouds, the mountains, water, air, and fire. When the mind showed pride, God controlled it by the use of His *Qudrat*, by the Light of His Wisdom, by His *Shukoor* [Contentment], by His Purity, and by the Radiance of His Qualities. He also controlled the torpor of illusion and the darkness of illusion.

When satan showed pride, satan was controlled by Allah's Good Thoughts and Good Qualities, by His *Saboor*, by His *Noor*—the Light of His Plenitude—and by the 24 letters of the *Kalimah*. God controlled satan's qualities and his darkness.

When desire—the dog of desire—showed pride, Allah controlled it by the use of His *Shukoor* [Contentment], *Tawakkal* [Surrender], and *Saboor* [Patience].

When the beasts showed pride, God controlled the beasts by sending Prophet Noah down to the earth, and by giving him Allah's *Qudrat*—His Power.

When the oceans, the creatures of the ocean, and the whales showed pride, God controlled the whale and all the creatures of the ocean by sending down Prophet Jonah—by sending him to the ocean and to the whale.

When the reptiles, birds, *jinns*, fairies, and demons showed pride, God controlled all of them by sending down Prophet Solomon (the Son of David) and by giving him Allah's Power and His Grace.

When satan showed pride, envy, jealousy, and the qualities hostile to God, and declared that he could create and destroy all things, God sent down Prophet Job and defeated him. He made satan surrender to the Truth. God taught satan that in spite of the number of evil things he did to Prophet Job, satan could not destroy God's Truth.

When *māya* [illusion] showed pride and claimed that there is no beauty greater than its beauty, Allah took a particle of His Beauty from His *Qudrat*—His Power—and placing it in Prophet Joseph, He said: "I created all beauty, but I did not create it out of My Beauty. I did not use even a dot—even a particle—of My Beauty. Oh, *māya*, do not show pride. Do not show pride in your miracles and magics. It is I who am that Incomparable Love and Undiminishing Beauty. In order that you may see this and run away, I cut one atom of My Beauty into seven hundred million pieces; and one particle of this was given to Prophet Joseph and his mother Rachel. That Beauty was taken from My Beauty. Look at this Beauty! Realize the Greatness of My Beauty. You are made out of the beauty of miracles, but this is My Natural Beauty." Saying this, God controlled *māya*.

When the idols and statues (which are the gods of satan) showed pride by trying to create an equal to God, Allah destroyed the idols through the agencies of many prophets, and He reduced the force of satan and the forces of *māya*, along with their *siddhis*—their miracles and magics.

When all of God's creations of the world were changed by satan and were made to worship the five elements of earth, fire, air, water, and ether; the sun, moon, and stars; dogs, cats, rats, and other forms and demons, God sent down Prophet Abraham. He had him thrown into their fire (which was their god) to prove that their fire-god could not harm Abraham. God showed this to Nimrod [the pagan king]. He demonstrated this to Nimrod by destroyng all of Nimrod's gods, idols, and *pūjas* [offerings]. Nimrod utilized all the poisons, snakes, and elephants to kill Abraham, but God made these agents to worship Abraham. By this He showed Nimrod that no harm can come to His prophets. By this He subdued Nimrod, his gods, and his idols.

91

When human beings sacrificed chickens, goats, bulls, and human lives as an offering to God, Allah demanded the sacrifice of Abraham's son, Ishmael. By doing this He made Abraham understand the amount of torment one goes through when sacrificing one's own son. Like this, He made it clear that sacrifices of all lives cause similar hurt and torment. God demanded that Ishmael be sacrificed by Abraham and his wife without the wavering of their minds. God said: "Your son must look at you and you must look at your son. Your wife must hold his head, and then you have to cut his neck and sacrifice him at the base of that mountain. Your blood should not quiver, your mind should not waver, your chest should not flutter, and you should not show any signs of bloodties and blood connections. Your hearts must not flutter. With stability of mind you should sacrifice Ishmael. He should be sacrificed in the manner I have described." But only Ishmael himself had that surrender to God, while the minds of Abraham and his wife wavered due to their attachment to their son.

At that time God told Abraham: "This is not the correct sacrifice. I have accepted your son Ishmael, but I have not accepted your sacrifice. Like the feelings that *you* had for your son, *all lives* that you sacrifice in the Name of God will have the same feelings of bloodties and attachments. Oh, Abraham! Your body is made of the five elements of earth, fire, water, air, and ether. All lives are made of the same five elements. Think and reflect about this."

Then God said: "I am now sending down a sheep to the place of real sacrifice. Sacrifice that! The sheep represents the mind. This mind is the place of good and evil, happiness and sorrows, and the craving of desire which nibbles at everything. That is the *nafs* [desires]. That is the sheep. If you can sacrifice these *nafs* from your heart, if you can catch this sheep of the mind and sacrifice it, then you can obtain My Grace. After this has been sacrificed through My Gaze, your food will become *Halāl* [permissible]." God said, "I accept and receive only the sacrifice of the mind, not the sacrifice of animals in My Name. Explain this to your people." Like this, you must sacrifice the *nafs amara*—the seven base desires.

In this way, through the agencies of His prophets, God subdued different things at different periods of time.

God sent down Prophet Moses at the time when the world was full of magics, magicians, and *mantras* [incantations], and when satan was being worshipped. Moses was given a staff. He controlled all the magics and magicians at that time. He then showed the people God's Truth and called them to accept the Truth. He destroyed the idols and all the statue-gods of satan, and he made the people accept only One God.

After Moses, the people of satan and the forces of illusion started performing *siddhis*—the miracles and magics of the 64 arts, the 64 sexual games, and the different types of healing. At this time Prophet Jesus was sent down to the earth by God, in order to destroy those miracles and to show how healing can take place through the *Qudrat*—the Power of God.

After Jesus, a time came when satan and *māya* started creating poetry, epics, *mantras*, and the *kalais* [arts and sciences]. There were tens of millions of different kinds of worships, idols, prayers, and swamis. They used to praise their gods by their poetry. They were also very well versed in astrology and astronomy. At that time Prophet Muhammad Mustafa was sent down by God, and God's History and the history of creation were revealed through God's *Qudrat* by the Qur'an. A challenge was made to all the poets to write a single line similar to that of the Qur'an. By the power of the Qur'an, God controlled all the poets, the poetry, the astrology, the astronomy, and the miracles. Having destroyed all the idols, and having destroyed all the poetry sung to these idols, He showed by His *Qudrat* the existence of God Alone, and He developed the brotherhood of man, unity, patience, and forbearance. Like this, God has sent down different prophets, at different ages, for different reasons. Over and over again, they have been sent in the different ages.

After Muhammad there are no more prophets. But there is Allah's *Qudrat*—that Power of the Light of the *Qutb* which is sent to the world. It can be described as Divine Luminous Wisdom—that Power of Allah. This *Qutb* continually warns the people. As that State of Wisdom, He shows the understanding to all. He shows what is right and wrong. To some He exists in the form of conscience. He exists in their conscience, in the Truth, in the Wisdom, in the Qualities of God, in the Gaze of God, in the Thoughts of God, in the Intentions of God, in the Justice of God, in the Conscience of God. He continues to show what is right and wrong and warns each one within his own heart. That One *Qutbiyat* exists in the world forever. If each conscience tries to understand this through Faith, Certitude, and Determination—through *Īmān*—His Presence will be realized. This *Qutb* warns within their conscience even those who have lost Faith, Certitude, and *Īmān* in God. He shows them right and wrong, good and evil. We must think about all of this.

94

These are the Laws of God which were revealed:

When the moon showed pride He subdued it by the dark clouds. When the sun showed pride He subdued it by the clouds and the rains. When hell showed pride He subdued it by the fire.

When man showed pride He subdued him with death. When the body showed pride He subdued it with hunger. When the mind showed pride He subdued it with Wisdom. When desire showed pride He subdued it with Patience. When the eyes showed pride He subdued them with Light. When the hands showed pride saying, ''This is done by me, this is done by me,'' He subdued them by the Hand of *Īmān—Nambikai* [Faith]. When the ears showed pride He subdued them with the noises of the elements and with thunder. He subdued them with the Explanations of Wisdom and the Sound of God's Truth. When the sounds of the world, the sounds of all music, formed the pride of the ears, He subdued that by the Resonance of His Truth. When the legs showed pride He subdued them with stones, thorns, heat, vapors, and different types of accidents. When the nose showed pride He subdued it with scents and bad smells. When man's body showed that pride of the self, attachments to relations, and bloodties, He subdued it with diseases.

When satan showed pride He subdued it with Truth. When snakes showed pride He subdued them with poison, lightning, and thunder. When the earth showed pride He subdued it with thunder and lightning. When the creations within the earth showed pride He subdued them with earthquakes and volcanoes. When desire showed pride He subdued it with suffering, poverty, and hardships. When the stars showed pride He subdued them with the sun. When the pride of the male said, ''I, I, I,'' He subdued that by creating the female. When the pride of the female said, "I, I, I," He subdued this by the monthly period.

It is like this. In every age God sent down Prophets to the earth. To control all the evil things that were revealed by satan, *māya*, demons, *jinns*, fairies, and by *mantras*, magics, *siddhis*, miracles, and the spirits created by the mind, God sent down each one of the Prophets with the Power of Allah. They destroyed those *saktis*—those energies or forces. Then God gave His Truth, His Beauty, His Plenitude, His Light, His Wisdom, His Grace, His Perfect Effulgence, His Qualities, His Duty, His Compassion, His Actions. He gave these to the Prophets and made them utilize these. In every age those evil *saktis* were subdued. Having subdued those evil forces, God made the Prophets reveal the Truth, and He implanted the Truth. Allah showed His Truth and thus protected His creations.

We must realize this. Having realized this, we must then realize God and His Truth and the Prophets whom He sent down to this earth. Having understood this, and having accepted this, we should open our hearts and give God that House. We must give Him the responsibility and pray to Him. This we should do. This is True Prayer. This is the way to reach our Father. We must reflect over this and realize this.

My children! Having understood this, you must realize the Explanations of our Father, the Explanations of His Gracious Understandings, and reflect with your Wisdom. Therefore, please search His Wisdom and His Qualities. It is only after we obtain His Wisdom and His Qualities that we can realize *Shānti*, True Peace—*Samathanam*, True Peacefulness. *Ameen*.

The Cell   I

Love. Children, who are the gems of my eye, children who have the fullness of God's Compassion and Love, my love. May God protect all of us.

My wonderful children, Man is a most wondrous being. Among men, within Man, God has placed many energies and strengths, many forces and many *saktis*. Man has these many *saktis* [forces or energies] so that he may know and understand many things. That is why God said in the past, at the time of the creation of Adam, "Man will know what the angels will not know. Man will understand all lives. He will be able to subdue and rule over them. He will be the one who understands all lives. Man is the one who knows all things. I have kept all My Secrets within Man and all of Man's secrets are within Me. Man is My secret, My Secret is Man. He will understand Me and I will understand him."

Out of all of His creations, He has given Man a very great title. Man has been given an exalted title. Why did God bestow this exalted title on Man? All other things have up to five types of wisdom, but Man has been given Analytic Wisdom—Divine Analytic Wisdom—which can understand right and wrong. He has been given the Wisdom of Light, the Power which can analyze what is right and what is wrong. His Grace, all of the universes, *awwal, dunyaa, ākhir* [the past, present, and future], the 18,000 universes, the oceans, the lands, the sky, the earth—everything has been given to Man. Everything has been kept within Man. One who has this Wisdom, one who is in this State, is called Man. Nothing else—not the angels, satan, illusion, darkness, or torpor; none of the *saktis*, none of the forces; nor the *jinns*, the fairies, the *devas* [deities], the angels, or the higher angels—nothing else can understand the secret of Man. But Man can understand all of the secrets.

Nothing else has the *sakti* or the force to understand the secret of Man. Earth, fire, water, air, space—none of these elements understand Man. They cannot understand Man, but Man can understand everything. That is why God has said, "Man is My secret and I am his Secret. He will know Me and I will know him. My treasury is Man, and I am his Treasury." That is Man. Who is this Man? In what manner did God create Man? My children, gems of my eye, you must try to understand what Man is.

God took one cell, a *nuqat* or dot from the letter *Alif.* Having taken this cell, He created the 18,000 universes within it. He placed the 18,000 universes, the 15 worlds, the appearances, hell, heaven, and everything within that one cell. He created all of the appearances, a limitless number of creations, and the four hundred trillion, ten thousand forces within that cell, and from that He created another one hundred and five million cells, and within these cells He placed the viruses and all of creation. All creations are in the form of cells. The atom, illusion, the world, the sun, the moon, the stars, fire, earth, water, air, space—whatever has been given appearance has appeared within that dot or cell. From this cell God has created everything else. Everything He has made appears from that cell. Dividing, adding, multiplying, subtracting, all is done from that cell. Everything that God has created—the heart, the lungs, the brain, the eyes, light, smell, speech, sight, sound—everything is contained within that cell. Through the cell, everything was created and given motion. The brain, the mind, the smell, the sound, desire, everything originated from the cell. Germs, viruses, atoms, creations, fish, the stars, the wind, everything, everything came from that cell.

In each cell there are *saktis* and forces. There are many forces in each cell. With this cell many different forces have been created. This cell can create many different forms of forces. This cell can create many *saktis*. This cell can destroy many things. This cell can create many things. This cell can eat many things. It is like this.

Blood is a cell. Sight is a cell. Water is a cell. Bone is a cell. Flesh is a cell. Each cell that works within each category of the body is a basic factor there. Each represents a basic cause. The whole world is a cell, and that which has been kept within this cell is called a *sakti* or a force. Even sperm is a cell. Torpor is a cell. Intellect is also a cell. Like this, it all exists. With this cell, many things can work. The work is done through these different cells. This is what is called 'creation'.

The cells come to the heart, and there they begin to work and to throb. The heart is the force station, the station that gives the force or the flow of blood. All of these forces, these *saktis*, can be created there. They are called *mano sakti* [the force of the mind], *māya sakti* [the force of illusion], *indira jalam* [the tricks of illusion] and *mantra jalam* [the tricks of *mantras*]. The cell does all of these things. Many things can come from one cell. It can draw all of the forces from space. From whatever section it draws the force, that force works in the appropriate manner. Through one's intellect these cells can work and operate according to various representations.

This is one aspect of creation. It can create blood, it can create *māya*, it can create the ovum, it can create destruction, it can create one that will eat up another. These are the cells which form this body. All bodies are formed from these cells. If disease comes, it is a cell. These forces or *saktis* are cells. What is spiritual is a cell. All of these basic things are cells.

But, my children who are the gems of my eye, this cell is creation. This has different *saktis* or forces. The One who created this cell, who created the energies which are created out of the cell, and who made it move and gave force to that cell is a Power. That Power is God. No matter how many investigations science may make—even if one attempts to stop moving things with this cell, with the different *yogas*, with different mental forces—it is just a cell. It is the force of creation, the force of the cell. All that would be analyzed is just the cell, the atom.

The atom is the cell. All of this is the understanding of the atom, which is creation and which is the body. What we see as creation, everything that is created, is made of cells. It is all atoms. One within another, one within another, one within another, one within another, there are many cells. There are viruses which are one within another, one within another, one within another. There are poisonous things and non-poisonous things which are one within another, one within another, one within another. Now this is the investigation in which man has tried to find out about the human cell. All that has appeared from these cells is called creation. Through this we can perform many *saktis*, miracles, and forces.

When one *sakti* is being performed, however, another cell destroys that cell. When that cell creates a force, another cell hits that cell. When that creates a force, another cell destroys it. When one cell rises another cell is destroyed. When one cell rises another gets destroyed. All creation came out of this cell, and this is how it works. No matter how much science or art you may learn, no matter what psychology or art or science you learn, whatever you learn, whatever miracle you try to perform, these are just forces which appear from a single cell. Each cell can destroy another cell. All of these miracles are at the level of the cell. The spiritual world is also a part of the cell.

But what Man has to understand is that Man was not created from that original cell. Man was not created from that cell. All other creations are made from that cell, but that Power which is called Man is God's Grace. That is a Power which came from Him. These cells cannot do anything to that Power. It is that Power which gives movement and life to the cells. That is the Power which moves the cell. The Power which can control all of these cells and forces is that Ray which is the Son of God. That is what is called Man, Man-God. It was not made from the cell. That is His Power. That Power is called Man, the Son of God. It does not have its origin with the cell. This body and all other aspects of creation have been made from cells, but Man is His secret.

That is why God has declared, "Man will understand Me, and I will understand him. He is My secret and I am his Secret. The angels will never understand this. The angels will not understand this." Man is capable of understanding what the angels cannot understand. That has no cell or form.

That which has no cell or form is Man, the Son. That has no destruction at any time. That is why Man is the indestructible one.

What is that aspect? That aspect of Man is his Soul. What is that Soul? That Soul is the Power. What is that Power? That Power is God's Light. That is what is known as Man. No cell can destroy that. That Power can control all of the cells. No matter how many forces or *saktis* there may be, that Power can destroy all of them. Those forces, those *saktis*, those cells, those atoms cannot destroy this Power. That is the distinction.

Because this distinction exists the earth is called Adam. In Tamil, it is called *Pārvadi*. *Pār* means earth, *vadi* means the forces that are found in the earth. *Pārvadi*. There may be good and evil in the earth. All of those things which exist as the forces of the earth are called *Pārvadi*. Adam and Eve, or *Sivam* and *Sakti* in Tamil, refer to the earth. The earth has four hundred trillion, ten thousand forces. All the viruses are found in it; all the cells are found in it; anything can be made with the cell. Things can grow in that earth; it can create things and it can destroy things. There is fire within it, there is water within it, there is air within it, there are colors within it, there is space within it; there are the moon, sun, colors, and clouds within it.

The cell is the world. The world is a cell. That cell is the world. That cell exists through earth, fire, water, air, and space. It works through these aspects. That is the world, a ball. It is round. It is a cell. This is creation. The movement of it depends on these five causes. Its darkness is the evil, arrogant qualities. That force—*Kun*! Arise!—came out of the forces of mind and desire, and it consists of seven aspects: earth, fire, water, air, space, mind, and desire. Within these there are tens and tens of millions of cells, and these cells keep on destroying each other, declaring 'I' and 'you'.

If we keep on investigating this, we find that Man did not come from this cell, but came as a Power of God, and therefore is called the Son of God. That Son will never be destroyed. That is the Soul. *Lā Ilāha, ill Allāhu wa innī 'Īsā Rūhullāh.* There is nothing other than You, O God, Only You are God. There is nothing other than God, Only You are God, there is another Prophet to come. Jesus is the Soul. That Soul is Jesus. That is the Soul, the Son, that Power. That is one part of our body. The Soul is forever indestructible. That is what is known as the Son.

This is the body; this is a cell. The physical body was made from a cell. One by one, each cell will eat the other. They are also creating and multiplying. One is multiplying; one is being eaten. There are many cells.

Therefore, children, gems of my eye, you must investigate. No matter how much might be learned, we have to think about this One Power. Everything appeared from a cell. Whatever we look at is a cell. From that cell, another cell was created. Whatever we look at is an atom, a cell; and from that, something is created. Whatever we look at must be seen through a microscope, and that microscope is the *Pahuth-Arivu*, Divine Analytic Wisdom. If this is analyzed with that microscope of Divine Analytic Wisdom, if each cell is analyzed, it will be found that the cell moves as a result of One Power. Therefore we must have Faith. Just because science says there is no God, we should not say that.

If there is an effect, there must be a cause. The cell has a form. Man's Soul has no form. To the Son there is no form, and the Father has no form. Both come from One. We can investigate all the cells, but we cannot know what kind of cell the Soul is. What form has it? What Power is it? We cannot see it with any scientific instrument. We can investigate the earth, the fire, the atom, the cell, but the Power which cannot be analyzed is God. That Power came from God. That Power can know everything; it can know what even the angels cannot know. It is a great microscope. That Wisdom is the microscope. When the microscope of Wisdom is used to investigate the cell, the existence of our Father will be immediately realized within it. How that cell moves, what it is doing, and how it came here can be known; and through the microscope of Wisdom you can understand that Power.

That Power cannot be understood through the microscope that scientists use. That can only understand the cell; it cannot understand what is beyond the cell. Therefore, when the cell starts moving, the force is inside it, and when it is analyzed it is realized that this comes from 'My God'. This is the Power which is moving these cells. Therefore, these are the reasons for us to understand Him through this movement, because Man is His Treasury.

We have come to this world to understand His story. We are His princes and we have come to ascertain the existence of God. You cannot look at a cell and say that God does not exist. If you do that, then you do not have the true microscope. You are also a cell, and that cell will be destroyed by another cell. If you think that your body is your self and that you are a cell, some other cell will eat up that cell. Therefore, that becomes a thing which can be destroyed. If man is to be one who is indestructible then he needs the true microscope. He was not created from the cell, he did not come from a cell. That is what appeared from God's Power. All of these cells have the forces of *māya*. Every force is there.

Children, gems of my eye, precious children, whenever you learn anything, remember that these are cells. The virus, the atom, everything is made from cells.

In the past there have been many *yugas* or ages. Every cell is a *yuga*. Every cell is a time period. Every cell is an appearance. Every cell is a basis. Every cell is a *sakti*. Every cell is a world. There is this wonderful treasure there. It is necessary to search with that microscope of Wisdom. When you study through that microscope you will then refer it to your Father. But for Him, not even an atom would move. No cell would move. Therefore, within that cell is His story. You cannot create anything.

Look at the heart, look at the intestines, look at the nerves, look at the marrow, look at a bone, look at the brain, look at a blood vessel, look at the fire. You cannot create anything that moves like that. Therefore, you must think about this. This One Power is the thing which makes them move. Nobody can create anything like that. Science cannot create like that. You might be able to repair what has already been made, but if the head has been cut off, you cannot repair it. You cannot repair it if the head is cut off. If the head exists you might be able to repair parts of the body. You might be able to do some mechanical work.

All that we see are cell forms. If a bullet is fired at the chest, on the side where the heart is, it cannot be repaired. It is death. Nothing can be done. We may be able to repair what God has created. But whether it is science or medical science, all that we can do is repair the parts God has already given us. He has already given us the material on which to work. It is only that which can be researched. It is only that cell. Simply because you can do that, you cannot deny the existence of God.

You have human conscience within you. No matter how

great a scientist one may be, when he is thinking, suddenly he might have a block where his brain stops and he misses and has to hit his own head in order for it to move again. While he is working a heart attack may come. Although he denies the existence of God on the outside, he will rub his heart and say, "My God, My God!" That is working within him. Even if he falls down, his conscience will say, "My God!" That is what it will say. Although he may externally proclaim that there is no God, still within him his conscience will say, "My God!"

God has given us eyes. Once these eyes are destroyed, we cannot replace them with new eyes. Because those eyes have been created, we have to accept that there is a Creator. We have to think with Wisdom. All have been created with cells—*maya*, satan, illusion, *saktis*, and forces. Each cell has a force within it. This is *maya*, this is illusion, this is *sakti*. Through the knowledge of these cells we cannot reach God. We cannot reach Him through the knowledge of these cells. Therefore, children who are the gems of my eye, you must reflect. Man has been created in a most exalted form. You have to understand who Man is. That Man is His Power. That is Light. That is God.

You can do *yoga*, you can do *gnānam*, you can hold your breath, you can perform magic, you can fly in the sky, you can do all of these things. The cell has this force within it. It has that magnet. Iron is within it. There is gold in it, there is lead in it, there is fire in it, there is water in it, there is mercury in it, there is oil in it, there is gas in it. All of these forces can work. All of them are found within the cell. Since these forces are within the cell, they can all be controlled. These cells can do that. We cannot reach God through this. We cannot reach that station through this, because this cell will be eaten by another cell. It will be eaten.

Therefore, this is not our life. This is not the Truth. This is appearance. This is creation. All that has been created is a cell. But there is something beyond this cell; that is the Son of God. That is what is known as that Power. That is what Man has to realize. When we go to realize that state, we have to find the microscope of Wisdom. When we find that microscope of Wisdom, then we can analyze it. God will be seen no matter what is learned.

We do not have that compass. We do not have the compass to show us the direction. What we have is the cell, the force, the energy. Because the force of *māya* and the cells of *māya* are within us, we do not have the compass to show us the direction for our journey. We do not have the map to get to that Point. Because we do not have the compass and the map, and because we do not know the way to God, we are left analyzing the cell. We are trying to understand the energies of the cell. Mind energy, *yoga* energy, *māya* energy, satan's energy, magic energy—we are trying to understand these *saktis*.

But that Power which gives movement to everything is Man, and that is God. This relationship is between God and Man, His Son. We must try to understand this connection between the Father and the Son. Therefore, once you and I understand this connection, we can control all these cells, we can control all these forces, we can understand all these cells, we can understand the nerves, the skin, the flesh, the wind, the direction of the flow of blood; everything can be understood. You must think about this. Having thought about this, having understood the explanation of it, we should then develop the Divine Qualities and the Divine Wisdom.

Gems of my eyes, children, you have to find a good

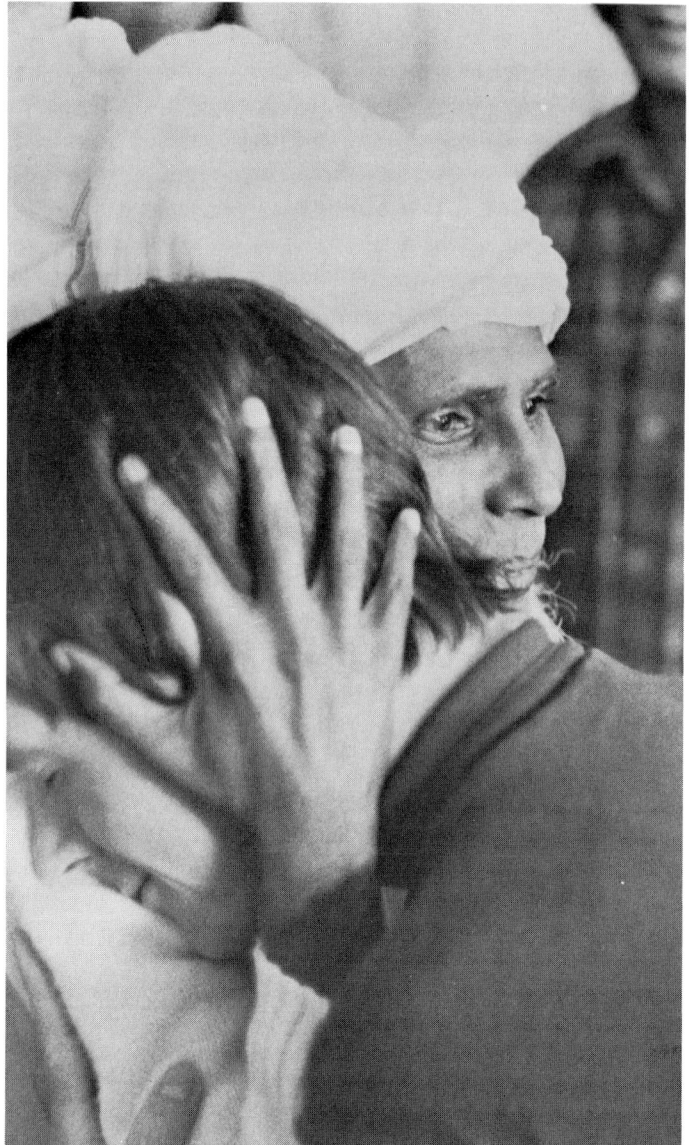

doctor. You need a good doctor. However much you may try to study the cell, you need a good doctor who has experience. Whatever way you have learned, whether from books or from something else, this cell has the disease of cancer. It is a dangerous cancer. This cancerous disease is in the heart. The heart is all of the cells joined together. The heart is the manifestation of the cell. Everything within that is cancerous. Blood cancer, religion cancer, wind cancer, all of these are within the cell. There are numerous cancerous cells within the heart, the cancer of 'I', the cancer of 'you', the cancer of 'mine' and 'yours'. All of them are filled with that cancer. There is the cancer of the 64 *lilas* [fascinations of the senses], the cancer of the 64 arts and sciences; it is all cancer, the disease of cancer. Cancer of the 96 obsessions, bilious cancer, 84 wind cancers, 18 anal cancers, 4,448 nerve cancers, 124,000 cancers of the small nerves—we are filled with these cancers. If we remove one cancer, another one comes. If we remove that cancer, still another cancer comes. If we operate on that, then the cancer of love comes. If we operate on that, then it becomes the cancer of property. Then it becomes the cancer of children. It is a very dangerous disease.

Therefore, the heart operation is a very delicate operation. You cannot operate with knowledge at cell level. For this heart operation, you must go to a doctor who has a lot of experience. When he operates, you will have to assist him in the operation and give him the instruments that he needs. You have to watch carefully every movement of that surgeon. As soon as he puts his hand out, you will have to know which instrument to give him. You have to learn from him and gain experience from him. No matter what you have learned on your own, you have to learn from an experienced doctor. You must take every instrument he gives you. You must take and keep all of the instruments he gives you. Having kept them within you, at the time of the operation when he cuts you open, he will put his hand out, and you must understand what he wants without his asking for it. He cannot speak because it is a cancer disease—blood cancer, cancer of the nerves—and he is covered with a mask and a gown. He cannot speak. He will teach you first, and after that you must have carefulness and attentiveness, and everything should be ready. When he performs his operation, when he reaches out his hand, you must know what to give him. When he does it one way, you will give him a needle. When he puts his hand out another way, you will know without his asking to give him the scissors. When he does it another way, you will know to give him the knife. This is how he proceeds with the operation. Before he goes on to the next step, you know what you should give him for this step. You must know what to give him at this point. You must know what medicine is needed for this disease. You must know that this nerve has to be cut in a certain way, and this has to be tied in a certain way. He knows that there is poison in this, and he knows it has to be removed and sutured so that the blood does not mingle with anything. You have to watch every step of his surgical operation, and for each movement of his hand you have to give him the proper instrument.

Through the doctor of experience this heart operation can be done. This heart operation is very dangerous. This operation is very difficult. If you take it to a doctor who has no experience, he will operate on all the cells and everything will die.

Therefore, whatever you may learn, whatever you may do, whatever you may have understood, in order to cut off this cancer, you have to learn that experiential learning from an experienced doctor only. Whatever you learn, you must learn it with an experienced doctor and know what instruments to give him, what needle, what knife, what scissors, and you must operate on that heart to remove all of the cancers no one else can remove.

There is a serious cancer disease. All the cancer cells are found there. Each cell is there, one destroying the other. The cell of the 18,000 universes is there. The four hundred trillion, ten thousand cells are there. They are all cancerous. There are one hundred and five million cancerous, poisonous cells there. There are 1,008 types of water cancer there. The 2,128 forces of the air, the spiritual cancers, are also there. The 1,008 fire vapor cancers are there. The 1,008 types of death cancers are there. All these cancers, tens and tens of millions of them, can only be cured through experiential learning under an experienced doctor.

We must work with that doctor. First, we have to learn all that he teaches. Everything must be absorbed within. When he takes you to the operating table and asks for something, that instrument has to be given. He will only move his hand slightly, so your sight must be there, your attention must be there, and you must know which instrument his hand wants. You have to move with a doctor who has this experience, and live with a doctor who has this experience. You must understand the practical experience of this and understand all that he does. If you do not do this, that cell cancer can never be cured. It is a dangerous disease.

Therefore, if you understand what this is and how to operate on it, then you can understand that cell of the Father's creation. Then you can understand the whole universe. You can understand the cell, psychology, science, arts, false wisdom, and True Wisdom. Everything can be understood. If you do not understand this, then every time you make an attempt to operate on this, that cancer will kill you. Each cell will destroy another cell, and finally it will destroy that person. Therefore, if you join with a doctor who has that experience, if you can study under him, realize and know what he does, understand every little thing, and learn this experience with him, then as he does the operation you can give him the instruments he needs. Then he can perform that operation very easily. But if you turn your head while he is operating and look at *māya* or at that cell or this cell, then the operation will not be a success. If you look at the miracles, the sounds, and the noises, then the operation will be a failure. That is a cancerous disease in the heart. It is spread within every cell. Because this operation cannot surgically remove this disease, everyone dies. Because it is a subtle operation, it is a difficult operation.

To find an experienced doctor is very rare. So please try to find one. If you try it will be good. If you realize the cell, creation, appearance, diseases, God, His Son, the relationship between the Father and the Son, that will be good. Please think about this. Whenever you understand anything, praise God. Please try to understand His history. Then this world will not be destroyed. If you keep on thinking of His Power, then the cell and the world will never be destroyed. He will protect that. If you keep on thinking of Him, then the cell cannot be destroyed, and the world will not be destroyed. But if you give up that Power, if you do not understand that Power, then the cell will be destroyed and the world will be destroyed. Why? Because the world is a cell and within it there are many other cells. And one day that cell will be eaten up.

If with each thought you know that God is the Power of that cell, then when you see that Power the cell will stop. We should always think of that Power in our thought, in our intention, in our Wisdom, in our sight, and we should always reflect upon that. That will be very good. That will be very good.

Please think about this, children who are the light of my eye.

Ameen. Ameen.

The Cell   II

Children who are the gems of my eyes, yesterday I spoke to you about the cell. We spoke about the cell, did we not? Those aspects of the cell represent creation. The *nuqat* or dot that was taken from the letter *Alif* is a cell, which is the appearance or the beginning. That cell, that point and its actions, gives rise to many cells when it becomes a fertilized ovum. The cells multiply and then differentiate. That is creation. That cell is the world. That is a round circle. The circle is the mind. The mind is the heart which moves as the result of five causes. It needs these five things in order to move and to have life.

The world moves by way of five causes. These five causes through which the movement occurs are enlarged by the mind and desire, which together with the five make seven causes. These seven causes are the seven heavens and the seven hells; and that is the cell. The cell is the seven heavens and the seven hells. Beyond this there is a Power, that Power is Heaven, it is God, it is not contained in the cell.

We have to think about the causes that move the cell. This cell is controlled by the action of each of these five, and that is the mind; that is this world. The body and the cell move as a result of earth, fire, water, air, and ether. Pressure and movement are created by the air, and by this process the five parts are taken in, the basic ones being water, air, and fire. These three are the basis of movement of the cell. The ether and the earth constitute the cell and are made to work by fire, air, and water. The air presses within the cell and this is the breath. That is air. With this air those aspects which control the air one by one—the pressures, the heat, the vapor, and the energy of the cell—can be controlled by the breath. That is air and with these airs these pressures pulsate, 'tic, tic, tic, tic, tic'.

If there is a wire or something through which air and the breath can travel, then if there is a 'dum', the air will stop. Then it will go again. Whatever aspect is brought to this force will move when the force moves. With the air the sound 'humm' of singing can go there. No matter what sound we take, it can go there. The sounds, the tapping and singing and music, can be heard in the wire. There are 2,128 energies in the air which can control singing and breath. With that energy the pressure of the air makes the blood ascend and descend. It can stop water, it will control the breath and the mind. This section can do all this. This control is done through the cell.

These five aspects along with mind and desire and this world which is the cell constitute the mind; that is the world. The 18,000 universes and all the energies which have been formed out of this cell can be controlled; they can be controlled by air, fire, water, the mind, and desire. As long as air can be controlled, these sections can be controlled. Air is the basis. That air is a cell. Within it is contained many

116

different sections which are formed in the cell. This is called *mano sakti*, or the force of the mind. It is called *siddhi*, it is called *mukti*, it is called *sakti*. These forces are described in this way.

This is the world and this is the basis of that cell. This is not the Cause of causes. This is not a very subtle cause. This is the explanation of the appearance of the cell. Through the force of the air you can control everything which appears from the cell. Through one cell you can control everything. This is not a fantastic energy. The functioning of this cell depends on the air.

It is like blowing air on a fire to start it. You use a bellows. It is like using a blower or a bellows to blow air to start a fire—it is not air, it is just a blower or bellows. There actually is no air within it, but when you press it the air escapes and when you relax it air enters. The air which comes from the outside enters into the bag and escapes when the bag is pressed, and when the bag is opened again, the air re-enters.

Like this, this mind and this body are like a bag. They are like a plastic bag. When you press this bag (which is composed of the five elements of earth, fire, air, water, and ether) with the breath, this bag draws the energy from the cells by way of the air. When you press the bag it draws in the energy of the world from the world or the cell. When the mind presses, the scenes of the cell, the point of the cell, the creations and sound are drawn in; they are inhaled. When you press again, the same forces are then released. The forces are released, then taken in again, and then released once again—this process is repeated over and over again.

This is how the formation and the maturation of the cell occurs. It absorbs the air and then releases it. This is 'spiritual'. The breath that is taken from the five elements, the cell, is exhaled back into the five elements. This is 'prayer'. When you keep on pumping this, when you do different types of *yogas*, meditations, or worship, what are you doing? Where are you taking the breath from? You are taking the air from these elements. That is your meditation. That is the cell. That is the world. That is the five elements. That is earth, air, fire, water, and ether. You draw the force in with the air, and then you press the same air out and give it back to the air again. You take the food from it and then you give the food back to the same place you took it from.

That food is called the *sakti*, the force of the cell. You take it from fire, you take it from earth, you take it from water, you take it from air, you take it from the colors, the ether, you take it from the world or the mind, you take it from *māya* [illusion]. By taking all of this within you, you draw in this meditation, and after pressurizing it you give it back to the five elements again. Fire and air are the gods you are giving it to, and this is 'spiritual'. This is 'meditation'—the blower, the bellows that blows air in and out. It takes in the air and then gives it back. But this is not True Prayer; this is not that Power. You are taking the forces from the five elements and then returning that food back to the five elements.

The cell also grows through the agencies of these five elements. It takes from the five elements and it gives to the five elements. This is what is called the bellows. The work of the bellows is like the working of the cell. This is the world. This is the way the cells manifest themselves and work with fire, water, and air as the base.

My children, the gems within my eyes, you should try to understand the basis of what I said yesterday. All the things which can be controlled by these bellows can move everything because the appearance came from the five elements. Therefore, you can move everything with air. You can stop air by controlling the breath. Once you stop breathing and control the air, everything is under control. That is not *yoga*. That is a cell. It is a cell which keeps on 'shooshing'. When you stop the thing which moves the air by pressure, when you stop your breath, movement stops. Then the five elements stop, the force of the water is lessened, the force of the fire is lessened. If you want to increase the force of the fire, or if you want to give more force to the water, then more air is needed. If you want to create blood, then air is needed. You need air in order to move whatever you want to move. If you can reduce the pressure of the air, all pressures and movements will be reduced. This is the cell which continues to control.

What can you do with the breath? When you say man can do everything—what can he do? This kind of doing belongs to the aspect of breath, to the aspect of air. But there is an opposite aspect which is called Light. The aspect of the breath is on one side and is called spirit. The other is Light. Light is the Soul. The Soul is the Light, the Truth. Air is spirit. These two are opposites: Light is the Plenitude—it has no control but it controls all of these things. If it stops, all forces will die. These are opposites. These are forces and this is a Power. The forces come from cells, but the Light is the Power. There is the *sakti* and there is the Power. The Power is a different thing.

They are opposites. When you breathe out, this control expels the air; and when you breathe in, it draws in the air. What is it doing? It is taking food from earth, fire, water, air, and ether. This is inhalation. Its whole life depends on this air. It brings in all these things and feels joyous. When the breath is pressed again and air is pushed out, it goes back to where it came from. This is the aspect of the cell. This cell

119

eats other cells, this cell receives the other cell, eats it, and grows from it, it 'prays' and it causes pressure, it controls all of this, it is the breath, the air. The section of this breath is like the bellows. It is the bellows. This is the world which is the mind. We must think about this. What can be done with this? It can only take the cell and make it grow. This is food for the cell. If you offer it your prayer, your meditation, your thoughts, the cell will accept and imbibe them. It will accept everything you offer. You can take whatever is there and imbibe it. You can give the cell only what you have. This is that control.

You can do any of these things with the breath. With the heat of fire you can do them. If you stop the heat, it becomes cold. If you stop the flow of water, the water flow stops. If you stop the flow of air, the pressure drops. If you stop that earth, it stops. If you stop the mind, all comes to a standstill. Then the bellows also stops. It is like this. You may think that man can do everything and that he can control all the *saktis*. I don't know! It is not like that. This is a broken kind of bellows.

There are nine openings or gates. The air goes in and out of these nine gates; the pressure of the air goes through these nine gates. There are two openings below the naval and seven above, making nine through which it goes. There are the two eyes, two ears, two nostrils, the mouth, the anal and urinary openings. These are the nine openings. The naval is the tenth, which is closed. There are two other openings through which the Power moves in and out. This Power is God. There are the nine and one which make ten, plus two equals twelve. These are the twelve gates or the bellows. This is that plastic bag. This is that bag of air; this is the cell and this is the world. This is the beginning of the cell, the growth of the cell, and the prayers. Whatever it desires it absorbs. This eats that and that eats this.

Therefore, children, you must think. Man cannot really control anything—that depends on the wind or air. Whatever man controls can be done. This is not a great wonder. If the air stops and you say, "I am a *yogi*," that is a crazy thing to say. When you stop breathing, everything stops. When the breath is stopped the sight ceases; when the force of the breath stops, the mind ceases; when the mind stops, the flow of blood ceases. To stop all of these is easy—one cell can stop another cell. This belongs to this section.

Therefore, you must understand that this is not prayer. It is like the bellows which when pressed blows out air. That is easy. But where does it take the air from? This air is really taken from the outside, which is the five elements of earth, fire, water, air, and ether. It is that air which is drawn into the bellows. When the bellows are pressed, the same air goes out and that air is then re-absorbed outside. Whatever goes out of the mind is consumed by the cells outside. It gives that to the cell and when the bellows are relaxed, then the air re-enters. It draws from the five elements to this body which eats it up. When these bellows are pressurized, all the prayers, meditations, *yoga*, and *gnānam* go back out into the five elements. They draw these and eat them. This is the point of the cell of the body.

Prayer is not this. The cell appears from there [the five elements], grows from there, dies there, and perishes there. But True Prayer is not like this. It is a thing that is cell-less, it pervades all the universes, it resonates, shines and resplends, it is that Treasure, it is that Power. That Power has no food here, it is not this air, it is not this breath, it is not this section.

Within the Wisdom which is the *Qutbiyat*, the Vibration, there is a Power. That Power is the Soul. It is God. That Ray which is Wisdom within Wisdom, which is a Light—that Light-form goes with a hiss, touches the Source which is God, and comes back.

If you press the switch here, where is that wire which connnects the Soul to God? If there is a switch here, as soon as the switch is pulled, the bulb will immediately light up. When you pull the switch of Wisdom, that Ray which is the Soul, that Current, that Power, goes back to God. That is where it shines and resplends. When you press this button of Wisdom, then that Power will be reflected in God, the Light. That Light will be seen. This and that are opposites. This Point, which is the Soul and God, is not the breath. God is Power. You cannot connect these two. That Power is not something that runs through water, air, and fire; it is not a thing that grows with the cells; it does not grow with the fire, water, and air. It is a Power. There are no wires which exist between them. There is a switch here, and there is a Light there; there is a Light there, and there is a switch here. If you switch this on, this is known; if you switch that on, that is known. It works automatically. There is no connection between these two. Whatever magnet or instruments you may use, you cannot find the connection between the Soul and God. If you want to find any connection, then you must have earth, fire, water, air, and ether. Only when we have these connections can a force be perceived; only when you have a piece of iron can you recognize the current; only if there is water can the current be recognized.

But none of these elements exist in That; these elements do not exist in God. There is no earth, fire, water, air, space, mind, or desire. They are not there; the world is not in God. Therefore, these things cannot touch That.

Only a piece of iron can recognize a magnet. Only if there is water can we recognize a flow of current. Only if

water is present can there be a short circuit and a fire. If there is no water, there is no short. Like this, the Power will recognize all of these forces. Since all things have been separated from It, since they have been filtered out, since It has recognized and discarded them, filtered and separated them out, that is the Power of God. It knows all these things, but they do not know It. Therefore, you cannot see God within the confines of the elements, the mind, and the desire. This breath, this speech, this cell, this water, this fire, this earth, this mind, this desire, this ether, the religions, and the colors cannot see God or be connected to God. If you take along all of these things, you cannot see God, that Power. These things do not exist in that Power because God has no form.

We have to find the switch of Wisdom. We have to discover that Wisdom, those Qualities, those Actions, that Beauty, the Qualities, the Actions, the Beauty, the Bliss, that Form, and Wisdom. We have to discover that switch of Power, God. His Qualities, His Actions, His Conduct, and His Duty are that switch. Only when you put this switch on will the Light burn there. When He knocks there, then this switch will work. Then His Sound, His Speech, His Beauty and all of those things that come with a 'tuk, tuk, tuk, tuk' sound will come.

That Power cannot be controlled by the cell. This cell is the world. Wherever the mind takes form, it must take it from the cell and grow with the aid of the cell. It only prays within the cell, it prays in *māya*, it prays from arrogance and in the state of arrogance, it prays within *karma*, it prays from within fire, it prays from within air. It draws from the water and from the earth. It is called *Parasakti* or *Pārvadi*. Such names are given to this *Paramesveri* because the earth is spread all over. The five elements are spread all over. This is

124

what we call the world or a cell or a dot, and all the things that grow within the cell are the things which it takes and prays to. What is taken in is what is given back.

Now look at a tree. There is a tree called the margosa tree. In that tree there is a *sakti*. If you or I sit under that tree it will draw out all the evil breaths and the breaths of disease within us, and pull it into itself. It pulls the carbon dioxide into itself. It draws it in, absorbs it, and gives out the good air, or oxygen which gives health. It takes in the carbon dioxide or the evil air and then gives you the healthy air, the oxygen. It gives oxygen, the air of fragrance, the healthy air. Once you draw this into your body, illnesses are cured.

Like this, the five elements and the mind take what they see from the cells. Also, when they pray they look at the cells. The mind looks at the cells because when the eye looks it focuses on the cells. If the eye sees no form, then vision cannot fall on that. This physical eye has to look at form. This ear has to hear sound, physical sound. Only in that way can we understand whether it is music or art. This ear can receive only those sounds. This nose has to have a smell, a form of smell which it can inhale—there must be fecal matter, there must be a flower, there must be fruit—the nose can only smell a form that gives odor. This mouth has to have food to find taste.

This mind has another kind of food. It has to have a cell, then only can the mind work. Like this, it takes only something that has appearance. If there is no form, the mind cannot pray, because it has to pray to a form. It will draw from a form or from a cell, it will take force from the cell, it will takes music (which is sound) from the cell, it will take taste from the cell. The mind can only draw from the five elements—that is the mind. Having taken them in, it prays to them. When it prays, it prays to them. When it prays it takes the force of the other cells. This is that force, the breath, the air. Whatever is taken in is pressed out like a bellows. That prayer which you utter is taken by these things. Like the margosa tree which takes carbon dioxide in and gives out good air, you take in the force of a cell, eat it up, and then return that same force back. That is the force. That is the *sakti*. That eats that. This is not True Prayer. We are praying to this form, these cells. This is called *māya*, illusion. This is not the State of Prayer.

There is a section in which there are no cells, no form, no appearance, and that is the Soul, Wisdom, God, the Light. You cannot pray to That with this breath. Within Wisdom there is another Treasure. Within His Quality there is another Treasure. Within His Duty there is another Duty. Within His Gaze there is another Gaze. Within His Action there is another Action. Within His Quality there is another Quality. Within His Light there is another Light. Within His Duty there is another Duty. Within His Plenitude there is another Plenitude. Within the Radiance, His Light, there is another Radiance. Within His Power there is another Power. The Power which exists within that Power exists as Wisdom, which is the Primal Effulgent Unique One. It is that Breath of *Imān*—of Faith, Certitude, and Determination—that has to be breathed. That Form is needed. That is Light. You need a switch for that. It has no cell. It is a Power.

It is said, *Lā Ilāha*, other than You there is no God. That Power is that Power—the other is the cell. The world is the cell, but that Power is not the world. It exists in the whole universe, it is Completeness, it pervades everywhere. You cannot control it since it has no switch—you cannot control that Power; it is not a force; it is Plenitude. You cannot stop it at this point or stop it at that point. There are different kinds of forces that come from the cell. That Power cannot be controlled by these forces. One cell will eat another cell. One cell can destroy another cell.

Now, there are germs in your body. There are 1,000 different forms of germs in your body. (Perhaps science has discovered about three or four types of germs.) If the white cells increase, the red cells will be eaten. There is another small cell. If that is in excess, it will eat up both the red cells and the white cells. If the red cells increase, then they may eat the white cells, they may destroy the white cells. One cell destroys another cell; one cell eats the other cell. The blood may eat it, the water may eat it, or the body may eat it. Like this, the cells can be eaten, one by another. These cells belong to that section.

But that Power has none of these *saktis* which eat one another. For example, fire will be consumed by water, or fire may consume water. Now this is not a great wonder. Wind might consume fire, and fire might consume wind. This is not a great thing. Water, fire, and air will be consumed by the earth. If you put water into earth, the earth will absorb that water. It eats the water. If you light a fire and place earth on top of it, the earth will eat up the fire. It eats the water, it eats the fire. These are the cells. Man says that he has controlled these with the cell. He says this can be controlled by that, and that can be controlled by this, and so on. This is 'local science'. The basis of the cell is not the basis of God. That is a different section altogether.

Above all cells the Ruler of all cells is the One who keeps the cells moving. That Ruler is the One who gives rise to movement within. If He stops, all stops. He is the thing which works without form, He is the thing which works without a cell, He is the thing which works endlessly, He is the thing which is beyond all control. It controls itself. It is that Power. This State is like this.

If you say that, with your breath and your mind you have stopped your breath, controlled this, or flown to the sky, what you are actually doing is using the five elements and sending this cell there. Other cells are eating this cell and then giving back forces to these cells. Because of this you think you can do everything. This is not Prayer; this is hopeless.

In Truth, we have to try to win the Grace of God. This is a separate section. It is His Form. Within His Form that Power exists, within that Power His Light exists, within His Light His Understanding exists, within that Understanding His Wisdom exists, within His Wisdom that Completeness exists, within that Completeness the entire universes exist. He exists within the entire universes. All and everything exists within Him. Within that He is the Ruler, within that He is the Trustee, within that is His Crown, within that is His Judgment, His Inquiry, and Judgment Day. Within that is that Power to create cells and destroy cells. Within that the cells and their manifestations exist. We must reflect upon this.

Having investigated this State, we have to understand it with clarity. We have to try to understand that section of God. Man has everything within him. He can control many things with air and breath, he can control various cells with that breath. This is not a great wonder—the ocean does this, fire does this, and various elements do this. This is not a big thing. A snake can coil around itself—even if you can coil like a snake, it is not a great thing because a snake can already coil like that. A snake might not have food for six months, it might live on just air alone. If you do that, is that a great thing? The snake does this already. You may coil like a snake and practice *yoga*, but for the snake that is a simple thing. That is a very simple matter for the snake. If you hold your breath and exist in that state, it is not a wonder. The snake stays in its pit for up to six months without food; for six months it might not eat anything, it might just hold its breath and wait there.

Take the whale, it eats only once in three months. It opens its mouth and swims in the sea. It has no digestive canals but it has a net in the anal region; and when it opens its mouth and goes *haa*! the fish which are passing by enter its body. The water filters through the net, but the big fish will be captured. The whale has a very large mouth. It might jump and travel sixty miles in one breath. The fish that are passing by in that sixty miles will be sucked into the net. There is no intestine, there is only a net through which the water is filtered and where the big fish are caught. Most of the water will be drained off, but a little water may remain. Once it fills itself, the whale rests with all the fish inside it. It drains off the water. With its breath, it expels the rest of the water. In the same way that the air leaves the anus, the water leaves the fish, and finally only the big fish remain. Then it closes that net in the anus and it waits. All of that becomes its food. For six months or for three months it will rest like that. After all this has been digested, and all the essence of it has been taken in, it does it again.

Now a whale does this. Is this a big thing? To wait in that posture like that is the same thing a snake does. It is not a big thing to control your breath. You say, "I will do this. I will fly in the air. I swim in the ocean." But the whale will take in all these fish and sleep in the ocean. This is not a big thing.

The peacock is an ordinary thing. You twist yourself in *yoga* like the peacock, you twist yourself like the snake, you twist yourself like the lion and the tiger. Is this a wonderful thing? It is an ordinary thing; the animals do this naturally. A scorpion bends its tail and its body and brings the end of its tail and its body over its head. Is this a wonder? You are trying to do what the scorpion does. You take your legs and your buttocks and bend them over your head and keep them in that position. That is not a great thing; a scorpion does this as a normal phenomenon. This is a very simple thing.

If you can bend the world like a bow and then shoot to touch God, that is a great wonder. That will be a big thing. If you can get into the Truth, that will be a great wonder. The other things are not a great wonder. The birds can bend their neck around and put it under their wing feathers. There are some birds that hold onto the branch of a tree and stand on one leg for many, many days. They stay there in the snow and the wind. You stand and hold your breath without speaking. A bird does this, this is not a great thing. All that you are doing is not wonderful, it is not a wonder at all. To do that which is wonderful is to bend yourself to that Power which is God. That is a wonder.

If you can merge with that Power, it is a great wonder. That Wisdom is a great wonder. If you can find it and find God, that is a great wonder. But to keep your eyes closed, to hold your breath, to walk on your head, and to keep on bending like different animals is not a great wonder. Even if you stand on your head the angel of death will somehow or other catch you. Whatever you may be doing, you cannot escape from the angel of death. Even if you are hidden in a stone, it will break through the stone. It will break through the stone. Death will never let you go. The angel of death will somehow come and grab you. So what is the use of trying to develop the body to that extent? What does it matter if you bend this body to that extent? Say you live for a hundred years, or you live for a hundred and twenty years, at the end of that the angel of death will come and the earth will eat up your body. What is great about this?

You have to find a *mantra* which will not kill you. You have to die before death. You keep this body with such care and attention—it is true you have to care for your body. If a company gives you a car, then it is your duty to look after that car. The car will not die with you. The company has given you the car for your journey. Now you can look after the car, but you also have to make that journey and get to the destination. It is you who has to travel in that car. You have to stop that car at the end of your journey and then speak. You have to go to that destination and then discuss business. You have to stop the car on the road and then go by yourself.

When you are going towards God the body will not go there. You have to stop it by the roadside, and reaching the destination you have to speak to your Father. You have to stop this body, and then you have to go past it and speak to your Father. You cannot carry your body and go there. That is why the body is given to you. You have to use it to go to your Father. You have to give your body to the cemetery. That is the place where all bodies or cars are garaged. This is only a basic vehicle for your journey, it is a rickshaw. This is a rickshaw, but you are trying to pull the 'trickshaw'. You are running it with tricks. That is where the fault is. Give that up and try to reflect that God has given you this body like a car for your journey. If you need to speak with God, then you have to park this body by the roadside.

You have to protect this body. Do not give it to a thief, and do not let it meet with accidents. But finally you have to go. You must go alone, not with the body. Who is it that has to go to the Father? It is the Son. It is the Son who speaks to the Father. It is the Son who rides on this body. It is a rickshaw. You must not make tricks out of it. Do not take it with you. Please think about this. If you have to speak with your Father, you have to go alone. You have to park this on the roadside. You cannot take it with you.

That is a path. There are four paths. Whatever path you may take, you finally have to end up in the cemetery. This has to be parked in the cemetery. Whatever religion it may be, whatever race it may be, whatever philosophy it may be, on the four paths you have to end in the cemetery. It is the parking lot. So, it is not a great thing to try to move your body or for one person to eat five peoples' food and drink 7 up. What is the purpose of all this? Whatever billboards you might advertise with, it is all just advertisements.

When we go to speak to our Father, we have to keep the body aside, and we have to become the Son of God. Only the Son can go to God. We cannot take this body and go to Him. You can look after it, you can put oil into it, you can put gasoline into it, you can put water into it, and you can maintain your car. That is a duty; to maintain that car is your duty. But your other duty is also to become the Son of God and to meet Him. You have to understand what section the cell belongs to, and you have to understand the section beyond the cell which is the Son of God. But to control your body or its movements the way that the snakes and birds do is not a great thing. You have not done anything newer than that.

Now the geese that come from here may go even as far as Ceylon or Singapore, and then they come back to Canada. Have you done anything more wonderful than this, or have you found a plane that has done anything better than this? This is what the birds have already done. All the *jinns* and ghosts and demons and fairies fly in the sky. They have also built their own houses there. But have you built anything? *Jinns* and fairies and demons exist in the sky, in the ether. You have not found anything very new. You say that you are going to build a house in the ether or space. At the time creation was made, these *jinns*, fairies, angels, and heavenly beings were already existing in the sky.

If you build a large tank and then put water in it, this is not a great wonder. The world is made out of these five elements of earth, fire, water, air, and ether. It is a big ball, and surrounding it is water. There is water above and below this round cell which is the world. There is fire above it and fire below it. However far this mind or that cell can go, it can only go as far as the water above and below. However much your desire might go, there is the fire above and the fire below. There is *māya* above and *māya* below. This is a ball, this is the world.

At the time that this world dies in you, then you will find God. When you do not have the world, you no longer have form. That is God, that is that Power. Otherwise, you are in the world or the cell. That world is the cell, that is an atom. It has been there from time immemorial. This is not something wonderful. But if you have found something new, if you understand who you are, if you understand who your Father is, that is a great wonder. That is a great wonder, and that is also very good.

Other than that, however much you may do *yoga* with your body, whether you eat buffalo, donkey, or whatever you raise and eat, even if you walk on your head, *'Izrā'eel*, the angel of death, will catch you one day. Then you cannot remain here anymore.

You must die before death. The cell always belongs to the earth. Therefore, praying through the cell, giving it to the earth, and saying that you control all these *saktis* or forces is not right. You have to think about it. You need to reflect. What you do is what the animal does, what the *jinn* does, what the fairy does, the demon does, or the monkey does.

You do what the monkey does, and you say that you have done a great wonder. The monkey will jump from tree to tree. That is not a great thing. Everything is in ether, water, air. Everything is there.

Just because you have gone from here to space, if you say I have taken water to outer space, it is not a great thing. You have to find out why that Power exists. You have to find out about that Power which circulates this water from the earth to the clouds and from the clouds back to the earth. It takes the sweat of the earth, and then recycles it from above as either mist or snow. What is it that draws this water from below and above and gives it back to you as rain or as snow or mist? What is that Thing? What is that Treasure? This is what you have to think about.

Like this, you have to understand the causes, you have to understand the basis, you have to understand the cells, appearances, and what the cell world is. But when you say that you are controlling things with these forces, it is just nonsense, because if your breath stops, everything stops. It is your breath that is the basis of the control of your mind. And with that mind, whatever you say that you want done is done. This is done. Please think and see. There is that One God. There is His Kingdom which is the Pure Kingdom. The Sons of God should try to understand His Pure Kingdom and Him. The cell is a part of His Story. The cell, the forms of these cells, look at each other and devour each other. They grow at the expense of each other. Therefore, this is not a great wonder. Where does your mind take things from? From earth, fire, water, air, and ether. It takes them from the five elements and the five senses. Having taken all these things within it, the air takes them in as breath. That same air is returned back to the five elements. When this is returned back, the five elements outside take in the air. This is not a great thing.

We have to understand True Prayer, the Son of God, and God. We have to understand the connection between these two Powers, the Son of God and God. We have to realize what that Power is and perform that. That will be very good. What is Prayer? It is Light. Prayer is Light. That Light is the Power. It is God. Prayer is Light. That Light is God, that Power. That Power is God. God is God.

This is what we have to do. That will be very good. Without understanding, whatever else we do is not really worthwhile. What you do in the world is not the tasty thing. The best thing is for you to understand and do that Prayer.

My love you, my children.

Go Within

Love. Children who are the gems of my eyes, my greetings to you. Children who are the light of my heart and my love, may God give you His Grace which you are seeking through your efforts, your intentions, your initiative, and your endeavor. May He give you that State, that Treasure, and that Grace. *Āmeen*.

This is a world of science, and you are the children in search of God. There are only a few in search of God. May God protect you and grant you His Grace. May He grant your intentions. May He give you all you require. May He give you His Qualities, His Blessings, His Fruits, and the place in His Kingdom for which you are searching. *Āmeen*.

Children, gems of my eyes, God is common to all. He is One who belongs to all. Within Him there is no 'I', no 'for you', no 'for me', or any such divisions. There is no such thing as 'my God', 'your God'. Nothing exists within Him that is for any particular color or race. He has no race, creed, or religion. Within Him there is no place for 'your religion' or 'my religion'. He is a Complete Faultless Power. He is that Impartial Treasure. He exists for everyone, from the baby in the arms to everybody. He is the True One for all creation. He is the Treasure of Beauty who exists without selfishness. That Treasure is the Form of Love. Justice is His Duty, and that Compassionate Look and Compassionate Duty are His Actions. The Treasure that has these Rare Qualities is our Father, and that is God.

That Treasure has no differences. He is the Treasure that is common to all lives. That Treasure will not receive anything from us. No matter what we offer, He will not receive it. He does not receive any portion of our food. He will not take our house, our gardens, our woods, our property, our candles, our lights, or our ghee. He only receives Compassion, Love, Truthful Qualities, and His Actions. He receives nothing other than this. You must think about this a little.

He is the One who understands the heart. He is the One who receives, having understood the Heart within the heart. He does not act one way outwardly while feeling another way within. He is not One who treats the poor one way and the rich another way. He shows no favoritism. He is not One who understands by looking outwardly, but He is the One who looks within and understands. He is the One who gives, having understood the *qalb* [heart] of each. He is the One who gives whatever is needed; what each one needs, He gives. If you want the world, He will give you the world. If you want heaven, He will give you heaven. If you want hell, He will give you hell. If you want wealth, He will give you wealth. Whatever you want, He will give you. Whatever is needed, ask of Him and He will give it.

Except for that One God, except for the Truth, except for His Qualities, except for His Actions, except for His Justice, except for His Divine Ruling, and except for His Conscience, whatever you ask from Him and receive from Him will be the thing that will kill you. He will give whatever a person asks for, but that same thing will kill that person. It will devour that person. Whether it is wealth of the earth or the skies, whether you ask for gold, a child, miracles, liberation, *yoga*, *gnānam*—whatever you may request, that very same thing will devour you.

After giving you what you requested, He observes you. The One who gives, watches. He watches what you do. It is no fault of the Giver. It is you who asked and it is you who received. You are the one who must carry the burden. It is not His fault. You cannot blame God. It is your mind, your desire, and your *nafs* [evil desires] that you must blame. Blame your eyes for it. It is the eyes that are a sore to us. Our nostrils are the things that cause our ills. Our mouth is our hell. Our ears are our illusions. Our mind is the house of *māya* [illusion]. He gives whatever you request, but then you cry because you are unable to bear the burden of it. Without being able to carry the burden, you cry. This is no fault of His. He has given you what you asked for, and you have to suffer what you must suffer.

When Wisdom comes, when you realize the Truth, and when you throw away the burdens that you asked for, then if you need your Father, ask for Him. Having discarded what exists within you, having discarded the burdens that you asked for, then if you need your Father, ask for Him. Ask for God. Then what He gives you will not kill you. That will be the only thing which will make you develop. There are four hundred trillion, ten thousand glitters of illusion, and there are one hundred and five million births. What you ask for will devour you. If you bring up a serpent, the serpent will kill you. The same thing that you bring up will destroy you. But we must blame ourselves for this. Please do not blame God—the fault is ours.

Therefore, children, gems of my eyes, kindly think of this and act accordingly. Whatever it is, think deeply about it. We have to eradicate our ignorance. Everything is within that One Treasure. That is One, Beautiful Power. That Beauty takes Form. That is the One which is intermingled as Love within Love, and as Wisdom within Resplendence. Truth is its Duty. Trust is its Life. Please think of this.

Do not grow beards for the sake of God. Do not light lamps for the sake of God. Do not waste your time for the sake of God. Do not give food for the sake of God. Do not decorate for the sake of God. Do not say God's Name for the sake of business. None of this is appropriate to Him. He is the One who is Complete in everything. Even before you intend anything, He has that in Completeness. He is the One who creates, sustains, and protects. He has no stomach. He has no hunger. He has no body. He has no form. He has no darkness. He has no torpor. He has no mind. He has no desire. He has no birth. He has no death. He has no beginning. He is the One who transcends the beginning and the end. He has no end. He is Omnipresent. He is the Unique One known as the Resonance of *ill Allāhu*. He is that One who is resonating, resplending, and shining. You need not alter any portion of your personal life for the sake of God. Do not alter your qualities, your actions, or your beauty for the sake of God. For the sake of God do not grow long hair. Do not grow a beard for the sake of God. You need not wear ochre robes or gowns for the sake of God. Such symbols are unnecessary for Him. He does not need a cap, a robe, or a crown. All of these are unnecessary.

He needs only the love and truth which is within you. You must give Him this. It is only this that you must give Him. He is an Almighty Effulgence. What is the use of lighting a candle for the sun? You cannot give the sun more light by lighting a candle for it. You must reflect. Why was the lighting of candles given as an example? As an example it was said, "Light a candle and look within your dark house. Your heart is very, very dark." The meaning of lighting the candle is: light this candle and see the darkness that is within your house. Like this, *gnānis* have given these examples and gone away. As examples they have said, "Light a lamp," or "Do this. Do that." They have said these things as examples and have gone away.

That is what the world says. Books say the same thing and religions also say it. But you must see the inner meaning of it and understand why it was said "Look within." The epics, the *purānas*, and religions say, "Light is needed for your house." You need Light for your *Atma*, your Soul. You need that Beauty to perform your duty. For the sake of the things mentioned earlier, please do not forget God. These things should be performed from within.

It is said, "Do not live in a city where there is no temple." The meaning is: you should not live in a city where there is no God. In fact you cannot stay in a city where there is no God. Nothing can live there. We must realize this. In a city where God does not dwell, there will be no rain or Benevolence. Nothing will move there. The meaning is: God has a temple everywhere. He even has a temple in the atom. There is a place for Him even in the atom. There is the Power which exists within all lives and that is the Temple, that is the Church, that is the Mosque. That is only for a few. It is for the people who will scrutinize within and observe. That Church is here within the *Qalb*. That Church exists as a place in which each can pray to God.

For those who do not have Wisdom, there is a different church in the world which is built of earth, fire, water, air and ether. It is decorated with paints and make-up. For the children in the world, it is a church which exists to give a warning and an awareness of God. You have to go to that church, go through it, and come out of it. You have to go to that church and give offerings, but they are not for God. They are for the people who are earning a living in the Name of God. The person who recites the Name of God has a stomach, eyes, hunger, aging, and death. On account of this, you must give him offerings; you must go and give offerings to him. You are not giving an offering to God. You are giving an offering to the one who is making a living in the Name of God. You must go there until your Wisdom develops. You must go there until this Church within opens. Until you place a Light here within, you must go to that outside church, not knowing whether it is wrong or right. The cage of your body is false. It is made of the five elements of earth, fire, water, air, and ether. The church outside is also made of the five elements; both are false. Until Wisdom develops and you are able to understand what is false, you have to go there.

When you realize that the church outside is false, you will realize that your body is also false. Both are made of the five elements, earth, fire, water, air, and ether. Both are false. Then you will realize what the Truth is. That Truth is the Point of God. It is the Church within which is not built of earth, fire, water, air, ether, or any of these things. It is built of the Grace of God. It is the Truth and it is within. The Form that worships is also within.

It is said: *La Ilaha ill Allahu, wa inni 'Isa Ruhullah* There is nothing other than You, O God. Only You are God. There is another Prophet to come, and Jesus is the Soul. That

142

is the Form of Wisdom, the Light Form of *Noor*, the Form of Truth. That Form contains the *Ruh*, the Soul, which is a Ray from God. This does not have a shadow. It has no form. It has no destruction. It can never be destroyed by earth, fire, water, air, or ether. It is His House, it is His Church. That is His Church. That is His Kingdom. That is the Heaven of God. That is the Form which He gives us which can never be destroyed. Until you develop that Form within, and until you understand the Truth of that Form which is the Son of God or Man-God, you have to go to the church. You will realize what the Truth is only when you realize what is false.

Therefore, children, you must think of this. Go to the church. Go to the mosque. Go to the temple. You must go. However, they are just to remind you and to make you aware of something. The lighting of lamps and candles are just examples. If you understand with Wisdom, and if you think about this, you will know that you must light this Lamp in order to dispel the darkness. In order to polish the heart, you must perform the Actions of God. You must have Wisdom and imbibe the Qualities of God.

What does the school child do? One child might bite the other, or might tear the book of another child, or might take the pen of another child and run away, or might beat the other. The teacher might spare his own child and spank another child, or bite another child and spare his own child. He might do that, that is the way of the world. The church is also the same. There may be many disturbances made by small children. There may be disturbances caused by teachers too, because they receive salaries. If there is no pay, what work has the teacher in the school or the church? Is it their fault? No. So do not blame them for that. However, because of that do not think that there is no God. That is the way of the world, that is how it is. Schools for young children are like that. That is to make you understand Wisdom.

When you understand Wisdom, when you know where your house is, when you start praying to your Father, when you search for the Light, when you go on searching for Beauty, and when you know what Love you must give Him—at the time you receive that Wisdom and understand what you must offer, then you need not go to the outside church. At that time, wherever you are is your Church. You already have the Light. That has been cleared and now you can unite with your Father. Therefore, you need not think, that is false, this is false. This is just one section of the four parts of the body. It is one part of the four sections of man. Those are four schools which you have to learn about. Therefore, you should not hate it. If you hate it, you have to hate your own self. Then you have to hate your body. You need not put on acts on account of this.

Has anyone seen Jesus? Has anyone seen Muhammad? Has anyone seen Moses? Has anyone seen Joseph? Has anyone seen Abraham? Is there anyone who has seen any of these Prophets? What is it that you possess within? Do not get angry for what I say. I am just telling you my experience. Just reflect on this and see. The forms you have retained within yourself are the forms of the arts. You are retaining what the artist made up for Jesus. You are keeping within you the Bible that the printer printed. You have kept within you the poems that poets have written, but are you keeping Jesus within you? You are keeping within you the picture which the artist drew. If there is a play depicting Jesus, a picture is taken of the actor. The picture of the actor who acted as Jesus is what you hold to be Jesus. It is the artist's picture of Jesus that you keep, or the picture from the Bible that you keep. For some it is necessary to retain outside pictures, but for others only the True Light from within will be accepted. According to the state of each person, he will see what he needs.

Truth must be with Truth. Then who is Jesus? Which picture is right? You must understand. By possessing this picture how can you ever see Jesus? With this Qur'ān that you keep, how can you see Muhammad? With this Judaism that you are practicing, how can you ever see Moses? You cannot see him, you cannot lift him. You are retaining what the monkey mind hurls at you. You make a form of that, and you keep it. Can you see Jesus or Moses or Muhammad with this? No. This is the work of little babies and children. What you have retained is a picture. This picture that you have is not Jesus. This picture of art is not Jesus. This picture of the person who performed the role of Jesus is not Jesus. This Bible is not Jesus. These are all poetry or songs.

But there is another Bible. That Bible is here, within. Jesus is not a picture. He is a Light. He is here. That is a Ray. It is a thing that has no picture at all. You cannot lay down that Truth. You cannot lay down the Truth. The Qur'ān can never be kept on the earth, because the earth cannot retain it. You have to keep this Qur'ān in a perfect store. You need a strong treasury for it. You need a pure, strong treasury for it. To keep God's Treasure, you need the Treasury of God. To keep the Light of God, you need the Treasury of the Light of God in which to keep it. In order to keep the Form and Power of God, you need His Power. That is that Church. You can keep it only in that Church. You cannot keep it on the earth, or on the fire, or on the body. You cannot keep this in any of these places. Therefore, reflect a little.

In order to hold that Truth, there is another Treasury. It is not the forms that the world retains which are artists' pictures. They are pictures of actors, but they are not that Truth. The Truth is extremely heavy. It is greater than the

145

18,000 universes. It is a Treasure which cannot be lifted by *'ālam* [this world], *arwāh* [the next world], or anything. How can you keep that Treasure on the table? You cannot keep it on the table. You cannot keep it on the shelf. You think you can carry it in your hand or put it on a table, but that Treasure cannot be carried like that. What is it that you must keep? What is the weight of it? What is the Power of it? When you understand, you will know that along this path you can realize your Father. There is no act for it. All of the acts have to disappear.

Children, gems of my eyes, you must think about this. There are many things we must reflect upon. This is how the Truth is. This is what God says. If we need to commune with it, with that Point, with that Truth, with God, this is the way we must commune—not with this form. If you want to speak with someone there, you cannot retain this form and communicate there. This form cannot communicate there. There is no form there. Only Light exists in that State. Only Light can communicate with Him. Power can communicate with Power. Truth can communicate with Truth. Plenitude can communicate with Plenitude. The Father must communicate with the Father. The Soul must communicate with the Soul. Wisdom must commune with Wisdom. Because of this, please think a little.

The period of destruction is nearing. Therefore, you must think a little. Do not waste your time. At the time we were born, we brought with us the 64 arts and the 64 *kalais* [arts and sciences]. We spoke millions of languages. What was the speech we spoke when we came? *Aaaaa, eeeee, ooooo, aaaaa, ooommmmm*—those are the sounds that we made when we came to the world. Our feet, arms, and legs were swimming. Although we could not move we were trying to swim in this ocean of *māya* [illusion]. Our hands and feet

146

were moving and peddling. Within a year we started making these sounds. During the first year we spoke all languages. We spoke the language of birds, the language of animals, and the language of man. We made those sounds, we uttered these as babies: *ooommmm*, *eeeeemm*, *aaaaam*. We made many sounds. We spoke these languages, and after one year we learned another language. The baby naturally speaks the language of the snake, the language of birds, the language of beasts, and the language of every animal. It speaks in all languages. That is the natural language of the stage where there is no Wisdom and where there is no understanding. The puppy speaks *aaaaah*, *aaaaah*, *hyaaah*. The puppy speaks all languages; and similarly, the baby speaks all languages. If we listen to the languages that children speak, they say *ooom*, *aam*, *eeemm*, *oom*, *aaam*. We hear these sounds coming from the mouths of babies. The baby will make the sounds of *aaah*, *ing*, *um*, *ring*, *uumm*, *ah*, *eeng*, *ung*. The baby will make these sounds on its own. Nobody teaches it.

Now what are you trying to do? You are trying to attain peace by making the sounds the baby made before it learned a language. The baby lies on its stomach beating its hands and feet and making those sounds. You are trying to repeat those same sounds. At the age of thirty, fifty, sixty, and seventy, after you have become adults you make the sounds of *aah*, *inng*. Now you are trying to repeat that noise of *ah*, *inng*, *unng*, *rring*, *ung*, *ung*; you are repeating these noises of *om*, *am*, *um*. What is the meaning of this? You are babies who have adult teeth, and you babies have given birth to babies. You are the babies whose brains have developed as men. You are the babies who are full of knowledge. You are the babies who are now learned in science. Now for the sake of peace of mind, you babies are making these noises of *ah, eee, um*. If you think of this you will say, "What wonder is this? At the time of my birth, when I was unable to stand and when I was trying to swim on my belly, I uttered these words on my own, speaking of happiness and sorrow."

Now in search of God and in order to reach peace, these grown-up babies are doing this. There is a lot of this in America. They are saying *am, aahm, eeem*. If anybody hears this, this is so strange it can make you dizzy. This is a craziness that exceeds the 96 other crazinesses. How many accidents are confronting us? How many griefs, how many adversities are we inviting into our life? For example, if fire asks for peace, it needs water to attain peace. When you pour water on it, what happens? Shoof! There is a noise like that and then the fire disappears. There was a man who wanted peace. He went to the tiger. The tiger gave him peace. It gave him good peace. He wanted peace; he got the good peace that he wanted. The snake went to the mongoose and asked for peace. It wanted to receive peace from the mongoose. The mongoose jumped once and cut off the snake's neck. The rat went to the cat asking for peace; it got good peace there. The cat went to the fox asking for peace. The lamb went to the tiger asking for peace. They all got peace, and we are searching for peace like that. We go and ask for peace from things that can kill us. Think of this and see.

We are humans. God has given us Wisdom and Love. God has bestowed very beautiful qualities on us. Man has the ability to understand even what the heavenly beings cannot understand. He has given us that great potentiality. For that He has the Justice which cannot be performed through acts. You must open your hearts and the Light of Truth should resplend there. You cannot see any of the Prophets in the form of a picture. You can only see or realize them in the Form of Light.

148

There are 124,000 plugs. Each plug must be plugged in correctly. If you insert it at the correct site, then sound and vibration will come. Telephone communication will come, television will come, Beauty will come. That Sound, that Communion will come directly; it will come directly. You can do that. It is easy. It is very easy. You only have to learn the correct switch and the correct plug for it. If you study the map correctly, and if by taking the map with you, you understand how to use the plug, then immediately you can insert the correct plug into the correct receptacle.

This is what we have to do. Having abandoned this, what are you doing? You are searching for peace in the world in the way we said earlier. The destruction of the world is nearing. The world will be destroyed very soon. All the people who went in search of peace will be dead. Everything will be over. Poverty is going to come, and you have forgotten the Truth of God, you have lost Faith in God.

Now I am studying ABC's in many books. I am learning the alphabet of *a, b, c, d*. In those books I did not see one word about God or one word of Truth. So far I have not seen anything about sister, brother, mother, father, family life, prayer, or the Truth of God in those books. So what can we do for that? Some time ago, when children were being taught in school, I saw that they would give praise to God and then start classes. I observed this when I gave advice to the principals of the schools. Children were taught to give praise to God and then start the lesson for the day. That does not happen in this country now. This state has now come.

You are not searching for God; therefore, in a little while the food from God will not come. You do not think of God; therefore, the Compassion of God will not fall on you. It will be like cattle eating hay. Distress will come and destruction will follow. You have no thought of God; therefore, the world is going to end with distress and fire. That state is going to come. When I look at this place, there is no room here to spread the Truth. Upon observation, it can be seen that they have made a business by giving the *mantras* of *aaah*, *ee*, and *um*. It is a business; *om*, *am* is a business. There is no need for God here. There is no place for Truth here. What you need here is a method of earning a living. There is no place in the world to teach the Truth, but there is room for anyone to conduct a business in the Name of God. If you put on the costume of a guru, there is a lot of business you can do; there is a lot of good business. There is room for such business people here, but there is no room for the Name of God. They are not teaching about God. They are teaching *aam, eem, um*. There is lots of room here for businesses, but Truth has no place at all. Therefore, when you look at this it causes great distress.

My children, this is how it really is. If you tell the Truth, the newspaper men will not accept it. If you speak the Truth, the television people will not accept it. If you tell the Truth, the scientists will not accept it. The radio people will not accept the Truth. The schools will not accept the Truth. The universities will not accept the Truth. Even psychology does not accept the Truth. The arts will not even accept it. The taverns do not accept it. Nothing accepts me. Even man is not accepting me. Now I am thinking what I should do. I am wondering what to do. This is our state now. Therefore, it is only God who must protect us. The world has come to this state. Therefore, my children, gems of my eyes, do not look at the world. Let us try to reach our Father.

May His Search be our search. May our search be His Search. May we give Him His Qualities, His Actions, His Love, and His Justice, and may He offer that same state to us. It is this that we must perform. Children, gems of my eyes, please try. Do not go the way the world is going today. Children of God must go on the Path of God. You must think of this, gems of my eyes. That is good. To search this Path is good. Each child, open your heart and invite your Father to come there. He is not a picture. He is a Light. Invite Him here. See Him here. Open this Church here. Search the Wisdom within it. Light that Light and then see your Father there. Put on that switch and receive all the Sounds from heaven. Receive the Sound of God, the heavens, and the celestial beings. Receive the sounds from paradise. If you can earn that Wisdom and if you can search His Qualities, then you can understand the Path. What we have to understand, what we must understand is His Treasury. Please think about this.

The world is a great wonder. If you have Wisdom, it becomes a huge mirror and a large television. If you can obtain those Qualities and that Wisdom, you will be able to see the entire universes and everything: the oceans, the lands, the worlds, the nether worlds, the world of the Soul, the world of illusions, the world of the body, the world of God, the world of hell, the world of the *jinns*, the world of the fairies, the world of the angels, the world of the *'Arsh* [the Throne of God], the world of the *Kursi* [the Eye of Wisdom], the world of Justice, and the world of the Power of our Father. You will be able to see everything in that television. You must know how to put on the switch. If you can do that, you can see everything that is happening in each of these worlds. But it is not seen with these physical eyes.

If you open this Church, there is another Form within it. That Form is Man-God, the Son of God. That Sound will come to that Form. When that Sound comes to that Form, when that communicates with that Form, it will come out. In

151

the same way that sound is emitted when you pluck the string of a violin, when Sound comes from there, it will resonate outwardly from within. The Sound of God will be heard outside like that. Then you can understand it here, there, and everywhere. You can understand it in the body, you can understand it from your heart, you can understand it from there. It is understood there with God, within your heart, and within your body. You will understand it in these three sections. Therefore, you must try to obtain this State.

There is no point in saying *ah, ing, ummm, om* mantras. These are the sounds that we made when we were babies, during a time when we had no Wisdom, during a time when we were babies sucking our mother's breast. This is what we learned at a time when we could not even stand up, at a time when we were swimming on our belly. Even the baby did not have peace at that time. That child was not in peace, it was just kicking its legs and moving its hands. It had a lot of work to do. So how can you get peace by making those sounds? Even when a baby makes those sounds it does not achieve peace. How can you get peace now if you say those sounds?

Nimmathi, in Tamil, means Peace of Mind. *Nimmathi* is *nil-mathi*. *Nil* means to stop. *Mathi* means to evaluate. In order to have Peace of Mind you must stop the mind through evaluation. By estimating or evaluating the mind, you can understand its birth and its end. Then after stopping the mind, you must try to understand it with Wisdom. Then you must analyze it through Divine Analytic Wisdom. After that you must investigate it through Divine Luminous Wisdom. That is Completeness which is beyond Completeness. You must think deeply about this and really understand. Please reflect upon each one of these things.

Children, gems of my eye, search for the Path of Truth. There is the left and the right. Both of these must operate.

The left relates to the world, which is the body. The right relates to the realm of the Soul. On the left you read the story of God. On the right you read the Power of God which is the Kingdom. You must understand both of these. To reach God you need not abandon the left. Do not abandon the left. Just go on marching left and right. When marching you have to raise the left leg and then raise the right leg. When you are marching, do not place everything on your head. Without burdening yourself with everything, just go on marching and perform your duty. Do not burden yourself with everything that you see. Just go on marching left, right, left, right. As both the legs move, do the duty for the left and do the duty for the right. Then continue to walk. There may be certain instances where you have to run. You will not be able to run with heavy loads. There are times when you may confront dangers and you will have to run away. If you have a burden, you cannot run.

This is how our life is. For the sake of this, you need not perform any act. You can go quietly. That is good.

May God protect us. May our Father relieve us from all ailments that are operating within us. May He remove all the diseases that are now afflicting us. O God, please protect us. May You save me and my children from all these afflictions.

Ameen. Ameen. Ameen.

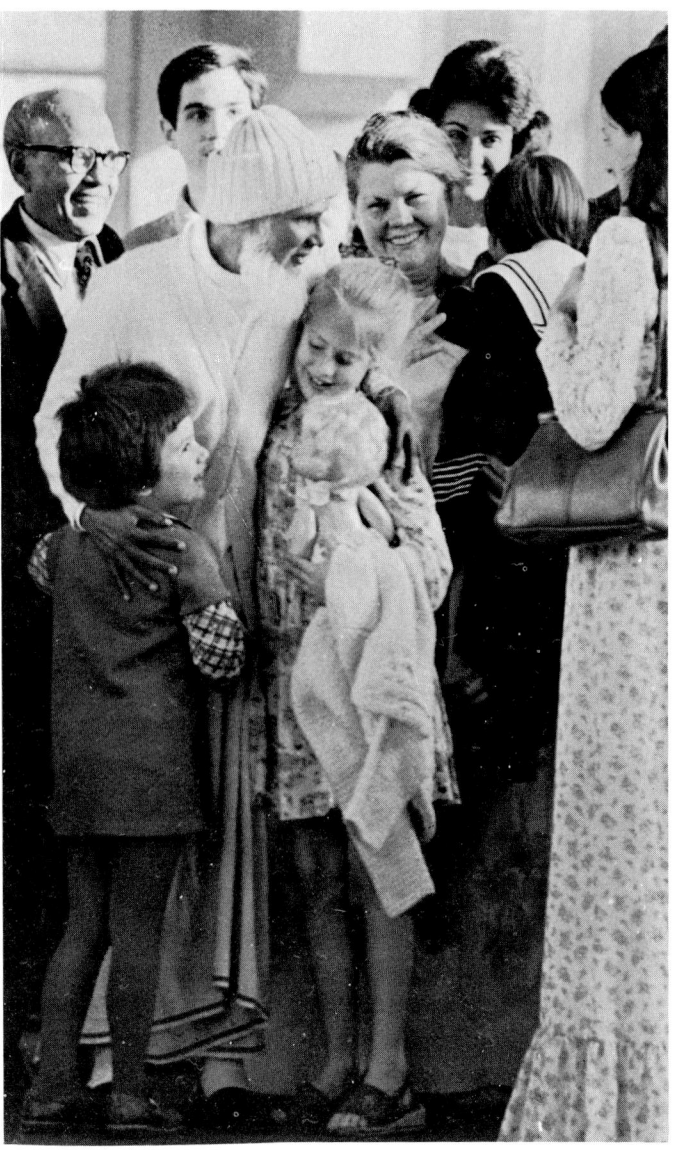

Come Forward

The secret of man is within God. Man is a subtle secret of God. For man God is a mysterious and subtle Secret. Man is within God and God is within man. The Treasury of the Truth of God is within man. Creation is within man. Grace is also within man. The entire Story of God is within man, and the story of man is within God. We need to reflect on this. God has given His entire Treasure to the bank of man. The bank of man's search exists within God. Man has to understand this. All the powers, all of the 18,000 universes, the Secrets of the Kingdom of God, and the secrets of the kingdom of hell exist within man. The Spotlessly Pure Church of God and the impure church of the evils of hell are the two different types of churches where worship is performed. The impure church of hell is where mind worships and enjoys the tastes of *māya* [illusion]. The Pure Resplendent Wisdom worships within that Divine Grace of the Kingdom of God. The Kingdom of God is the Place of

155

Prayer to our Father. If these two explanations are understood, then man can realize Peace. He can understand what Peace is for man.

God has given every section to man. He has displayed His Story in each one of these actions as books. All these books are found in His section of creation. These are all the books which tell the Story of God. All that the mind sees, all that the nose smells, all that the brain realizes, all that the ear hears, all that the speech speaks, all that the tongue tastes, all that the body feels, all that desire realizes, and all that the Light of Wisdom which is the *Zāt* or Essence of God realizes—all are His Story. It is only the Light of Wisdom, the *Zāt*, that sees His Complete Story with clarity. It is this Wisdom that separates, analyzes, and extracts the Truth from this Story.

The section that relates to the earth, the section that relates to the vapors, the section that relates to the five elements (earth, fire, water, air, and ether), the section that relates to *māya*, the section that relates to the darkness of satan, the section that relates to the monkey mind, and the section that relates to the dog of desire are realized, understood, and analyzed by Wisdom. It discards what has to be discarded. It analyzes and discards all of the sections that relate to darkness and torpor. It researches and looks into the cells and the atoms. It extracts only the Truth from these books. Wisdom extracts the Truth from the entire creation and discards all that relates to hell, to the world, to the elements, to the senses, to illusion, to *māya*, to the mind, and to the dog of desire. It discards all of these sections and retains only that one section which is that Beautiful Form of that Power of His Grace. It is like a filter that filters out everything except that One Power which knows no destruction. This Power cannot be destroyed by the elements. Nothing can destroy this Power. Wisdom extracts this Power. It looks at this One Power and understands this as 'My God'. Wisdom then surrenders to this One Power known as God. This is the One Point for Man.

Wisdom also realizes that God has given His entire Powers to man. If man understands this, if he closes the doors of all of the business shops that relate to the left, and if he develops that indestructible Treasure of the Kingdom of God which is on the right, then he will not have any want or need. He will not experience any difficulties, sorrows, unhappinesses, or distresses. He will not have any of these. Since everything is within him, he may take whatever he needs. Because he can extract whatever he needs and utilize it, there is no sorrow, unhappiness, or distress for him.

Man does not think about this. Man does not think of this Wisdom and these Treasures. It is because man does not know this that he experiences grief and sorrow. This is why he has no peace. This is why he has no happiness. And this is why he experiences birth, death, unhappiness, and difficulties. Man does not realize that it is he who has caused his own suffering. He possesses the bank within himself. He had the key to open that bank, but he has thrown it away. He has lost the key to that bank, and he goes on feeling the bank with his ignorance. Now he blames the One who created and deposited that bank within him. He denies God and asks questions such as, "Why was I created?" He says, "Because things are like this, there is no God." He does not realize that this is his own fault. When he is in this state, a warning comes to him.

After the Prophets, there is a state of Wisdom called the *Qutb*. From His Seat of Justice the *Qutb* warns or monitors to man in the four different ways of God's Justice: The Divine Justice of God, which warns that you are the ruler for your

157

body and your mind; the king's justice; human justice; and human conscience. These four states of justice within man will at certain moments monitor to him and say, "Do not blame God. You must realize the Truth within yourself." It warns him, saying, "See whether what you have done is right or wrong." The *Qutbiyat* automatically warns from within. Finally the conscience warns him and says, "You are denying God. What you have done is wrong. It is wrong that you beat him. It is wrong that you scolded him. You have killed someone. That is wrong." The conscience warns him and makes him aware of his actions. It tells him, "God will question you for this one day. Go and apologize for this." It makes him feel sorry and it makes him think about what has happened. It makes him grieve and regret what he had done. In this state he is aware of this. However, even then man only realizes this for a second, the next second he forgets.

He acts like the turtle that dwells in the sea and the frog that dwells in the pond. Man comes out of the ocean of illusion where he lives and basks in the Light of Truth. Just as the turtle dwelling in the sea and the frog that lives in the pond come out for a moment to bask in the warmth of the sun, the mind and the desire of man, which dwell in the ocean of *māya*, come out for a moment and bask in the Light of God. The meaning of this is: the turtle, which represents the mind, comes out of the ocean and goes to the shore, lays a thousand eggs, covers them up with the sand, and then goes back into the ocean again. Like this, the mind of man comes out of the ocean of illusion, lays a thousand eggs in a second, and then goes back into the ocean of *māya* again. These thousands and thousands of eggs hatch on the shores of the ocean of illusion, and these thousands and thousands multiply within the mind. What are these eggs that are hatched within the mind? They are the qualities of jealousy, pride, arrogance, and the differences of 'you' and 'I'. Like this, all of the eggs of the evil qualities are hatched. When these eggs are hatched, they multiply all of the qualities of satan and the glitters of *māya*. These eggs of ignorance hatch and spread all of the evil qualities. Once these eggs are hatched, they again return to the ocean of illusion, which is the mind. What hatched on the shores of illusion again returns to the ocean of *māya*. Like that, they go on multiplying. They go on multiplying in geometrical progressions. It is the nature of the mind to hatch and multiply in this way.

Just as the turtle comes out of the ocean and enjoys the sun, the mind of man also comes from the ocean of illusion to bask in the Light of God. Divine Wisdom, which is the *Qutb*, comes and monitors to him. At that moment he thinks and reflects. The *Qutb*, which is that Divine Light, prompts: "Just think. Do you not need this Light? Do you not need this Justice? Do you not need this Truth? Come forward! Just leave the place where you are! Just come forward a little. Leave the place where you are! Come forward. Leave the ocean and come out!" When the *Qutb* says this, the turtle immediately goes back into the ocean. Again it goes back into the ocean. This is not the fault of God. It repeats the same thing again. It lays its own eggs and goes on suffering. This is the way of the mind. This is the mind. Without listening to the warning, it goes on repeating what it did before. Whose fault is this? Is this the fault of God? No! It is not the fault of God. This is the fault of the monkey mind. It is the fault of the elements. It is because man has discarded his Wisdom. It is because he has lost the key to the bank of the Treasury of God. This is not the fault of God. God has given everything, but man is like this turtle. He has fallen into the mind, he has fallen into the turtle of jealousy, and he continues to live

159

within it. Because he continues to live in it, he suffers. This is not the fault of God.

The frog represents desire. That frog of desire also comes out of the pond when it is warned by the conscience. When the frog of desire experiences suffering, it comes out of the pond. Then when the *Qutb*, which is Divine Luminous Wisdom, questions, "Ah, have you come out? Come here. Come forward a little." He says: "God has given you everything. You have been croaking all of the time inside the water. You have been croaking day and night while you were in the water. And upon seeing the rain, you have also been croaking day and night. You were so happy to see this magic rain of appearances, and the births and deaths of creation. For the sake of food, for the sake of the blood, for the sake of desire, for the sake of pleasures, and out of desire for that one cell, over and over again you have been croaking. Each sound that came out of your mouth has become eggs. All of your saliva has become eggs. All your intentions have become eggs. You have laid these eggs over such a long distance. These are all tadpoles of desire. You have been shouting and croaking night by night, and now you are almost dead. You have been croaking and making a lot of noise at night. But in the morning, the stork or eagle will catch hold of you and run away. You have hatched all of these things, but what have you gained? The next day you will fall prey to either the stork or the eagle.

The *Qutb* then says, "O frog of desire, you are always shouting with your mouth, but you are really hatching evil. This will lead you to death and nothing else. This is the *karma* that you are multiplying in this pond. Come here, come out of that pond. There are a lot of good things here. Come, come let us walk. There is good light here. There is no evil here." The frog listens to everything, shakes its head,

160

and again jumps back into the pond. It jumps back into the pond, croaks again, and dies. Having hatched all the evils, the frog dies. Is this the fault of God? Even though Wisdom warned and advised the frog, it did not listen. Therefore, man must think and reflect on this. It is like this that man's mind and desire take the earth, fire, water, air, and ether and make these his entire life. He takes the arrogance of the 'I' into him, and he blames God for the consequences. God has given everything to man. He blames God and says, "I have no peace of mind." How can peace be given to the mind that has hatched so much evil in this ocean of *māya*? When this frog of desire has hatched so many, many thousands of eggs of desire, how can peace come? Peace will never come. If he wants peace, he must come to the place where peace exists. If he understands this place, then there is peace. But man does not realize this. Without understanding or realizing this through his Wisdom, he even denies God. Man has to reflect on this. He must really reflect to see where peace exists.

Man must think. God has given everything to man. But the world and man blame God saying, "Why did God create me? He has not given me that. He has not given me this. He has not given me that." But God has given everything. He has given man a place in order that he may live in peace. He has given the Treasure in order to obtain peace. All that is needed has been given to man. Man has discarded this.

Just observe the skies; there are four seasons, summer, autumn, winter, and spring. These are the four seasons. There is earth which shakes, there is the flow of water, there is the section of fire, and there is the section of air. There are these four sections. In the same way that these exist, man has four seasons. There are four seasons in the human body: the sections of earth, fire, water, and air. Sometimes these four sections change. As one goes, the other comes. As

161

the other comes, another goes. Like this, they may follow one another.

The entire creation of God is a farm. As seasons change there will be rain. During one season, water is taken from the ocean to the clouds and is again deposited as rain on the world. And then when the rain falls, ponds, lakes, and tanks will be filled. Then the earth draws in water and the remaining water flows back to the oceans or rivers. Man is depending on this rain water in order to plow his land and reap his harvest. But during the seasons when there is no rain, he blames God. He blames God because there is no rain. He says, "There is no water, we cannot plow. What kind of God is this?" Is this the fault of God? It is not the fault of God. This is the fault of the seasons. Each section is working according to what it naturally does. These four sections of earth, fire, water, and air are working according to their natural sections. They are performing their duty. Even though each of these sections is performing its own duty, man blames God. This is not the fault of God, these are the seasonal changes.

Man has been given a natural source of water. He must think of this. There is water in the earth up to the sea level. But he has to dig there in order to obtain this water. Just as the water was stored up, and just as he thought of farming and getting produce according to seasonal changes, he also accumulated a house, property, wife, children, and worldly possessions. He accumulated and stored up differences of races, sects and religions, illusions, selfishness, jealousy, arrogance, and envy. He was waiting for the rain of *māya*. He built up all these things and was waiting for the rain of illusion. But there is no satisfaction in these things. Sometimes there will be sorrow, and sometimes there will be happiness. Like that, whatever man has collected will give

162

him sorrow as well as happiness. These are not permanent things. This is not the spring water for his farm. These are not things that will help him permanently.

In order to perform the cultivation of *māya,* man builds a reservoir of *māya* to collect all that he wants. When it is full, it will give him both sorrow and happiness. At one moment he will laugh, and at a thousand moments he will cry. He will laugh and afterwards he will cry. This is not the fault of God. There is a spring which God has given him naturally. He must find and obtain this spring water. He should not find fault with God. Just as he endeavours to build the reservoir for *māya,* he must dig for the Truth. Man should use his Wisdom to dig for and open that spring within. If he had opened that spring water within during the time that he spent building up the qualities of *māya* and waiting for the rain of illusion, then he would have opened the Springs of the *Rahmat* [Benevolence] of God. If he digs to the sea level, if that Fountain of Grace opens, if the eyes of that Fountain open, then there will be Eternal Water for man. He need not depend on time and seasons. He can cultivate at all times and there will be happiness forever. At all times there will be crops. Whether the rain falls or not, there will be crops; whether the sun comes out or not, there will be crops; whether the seasons change or not, there will be crops. This will be an Eternal Crop. Then he will have Eternal Peace.

He has to open that Spring Water. If man opens the spring of his Soul with the Key of his Wisdom and extracts the Benevolence of that bank, that is the Grace that will quench his thirst. That is the water for the Soul. That is the Treasure which will make the Soul grow. That is the Light to reach God, the Father.

Instead of doing this, man blames God. But whose fault is this? Having discarded this state of Peace, man searches for peace. He says *mantras* such as *aaim, om, aam, riiyim, kiyim, iyim, ayim, kilium,* and *savum.* He continues to recite such *mantras,* he recites many *mantras.* At the time when he was a baby, he made these sounds. Babies make such sounds as these *mantras* before they are able to sit up. Like this, there are four hundred trillion, ten thousand bird sounds, animal sounds, air sounds, and water sounds made by the babies. Babies make these sounds while trying to crawl on their stomachs and before they are able to stand up.

Now adults, who are mature in age, who are mature in learning, whose brains are mature, whose teeth are mature, and whose hair has become grey, are repeating these same sounds. They have progressed in intellect and have become mature in age, but they are again repeating the *mantras* of babies. Repeating these *mantras,* they are trying to find peace. This is really a wonder. While searching for peace, such a one grabs hold of a tiger. He falls at the feet of the tiger and then asks for peace. The tiger gives peace by devouring him. He becomes a rat and asks for peace from the cat. The cat devours him and gives him peace. He becomes a snake and goes to the mongoose and asks for peace. He becomes a lamb and goes to the lion and asks for peace. He becomes a bird and goes to the dog and asks for peace. He becomes a bull and goes to the lion and asks for peace. He becomes a monkey and asks the tiger to give him peace. He becomes an insect and asks the cat for peace. He becomes a fish and goes to the fire and asks for peace. He becomes a donkey and goes to the rhinoceros and asks for peace.

Like this, utilizing many thousands and thousands of qualities that he has developed as a result of discarding his Wisdom, man goes to the elements of earth, fire, water, air, ether, mind, and desire and asks for peace. He uses the qualities of satan and he asks for peace. He asks for peace from the darkness of satan, which leads to one hundred and five million births. He discards the intellect and goes to these energies in search of peace. Man goes in search of peace of mind to these energies. These will never give him peace. These qualities will only kill man, but they will never give him any peace. Man must think about this. He must reflect and understand this.

The Treasures that God has given to man must be understood. Man must understand and know who God is. Man must understand God's Treasury. He must realize that Man is the Son of God. God is within man, and man is within God. This unity must be understood. Man has to understand the point of how he can live in unity with God. Man is God's secret, and God is man's Secret. Man is God's bank, and God is man's Bank. Man is the one who plows, grows, and displays the Story of God, and man's story is displayed by God. It is man who has this state of beauty and this state of exaltedness. To man this Treasure is his Peace. If man can understand this state of Wisdom and this Treasury, then he is the Son of God. Whatever is needed he will get. There is nothing else that he needs. He will never be in need. He will be the ruler for the Kingdom of God. He will be the Prince of God. He will be the one who has earned the Crown of God. He will have earned the Kingdom of God which exists everywhere. Then all of the universes are his kingdom, and everything there belongs to him. He will have no needs, because everything that can be understood will be for the Prince of God.

The kingdom of hell is just one cell. That is the world of illusion, that is the world of desire, that is the world of satan. That is the world of creation, that is the earth, fire, water, air, ether, mind, and desire. That is the world of darkness, and that is the world of *māya*. Its crops are found in the world of hell. It originates from just a small cell. This world of hell is just one small cell. There is a great difference between the extent of the Kingdom of God and the kingdom of hell. What has been discarded from the Kingdom of Heaven has been placed in this one cell of hell. All that has been completely filtered off from heaven is deposited in this one cell of hell. The Original is contained in Heaven. The heart is the bank and the treasury for man. God's Power and Grace exist there. That is His Kingdom. If man understands and realizes what the kingdom of hell is and what the Kingdom of Heaven is, he will realize that there will never be peace in that cell. Peace exists only in that Treasury which is the Kingdom of Heaven. There will never be peace in mind and desire. Peace exists in His Truth and and His Wisdom. Peace exists in that Treasury of God. It can never be found within this cell. Man should be aware of this.

You need light to dispell darkness. In the same way, one needs Wisdom to dispell the darkness of the mind. If this Light is absent that house will always be dark, and man will not know the Treasure which he possesses within. He will continue to go on feeling in the dark. And when he goes on feeling, he is without peace. Only if there is Light can someone see and take what is there. Therefore, man must try to obtain that Truth, which is the Truth of Light.

My children, please think about this. Open that Treasury, from there you can obtain peace. That Treasury will give you peace.

Ameen.

The Soul

My Love. My children who are the gems of my eyes, children who are the loving children of God, may God protect you. May He take us along that Path so that we may reach Him. May His Help and His Benediction be showered upon us. May that King who is the Creator and Protector protect us in this world and the next world. May He protect us in our high states and in our low states. May He carry us in His Hands and support us.

My children, who are the gems of my eyes, this is our birth. We call this our birth. Our thoughts, our looks, the sounds in our ears, the scent in our nose, the speech in the mouth, the runnings of the mind, the intentions of the body, and our ideas are all formed within the body. As a result of the formation and appearance of these things and these actions, we think that we are men. There is a state of Peace between God and Man, there is a state of Peace between Man and God. There is a connection between God and Man.

This has been created within Man. There is also a state of desire and craving that exists as a connection among satan, *māya* [illusion], and the mind. Sometimes people call that 'peace of mind', they call this state 'peace of mind'. The other aspect is also called Peace of Mind, but one is a negative aspect and one is a positive aspect. Man has to understand which peace should be attained and through which source he should be able to attain peace. It is only then that the true state of Peace can be realized.

When you talk about peace of mind, that true state of Peace and those connections which bring about Peace of Mind should be understood. Does *māya* give Peace, or is it the connection with God that gives Peace? These two states should be understood. One is the state of Peace with God and with the Soul. This is the state of the *Qalb*, which is the Flower of the Heart. The other state that is called peace of mind is the section of *māya*. There are two states, one is Peace of the Soul, the other is peace of mind. We should try to understand which state of peace we are searching for. Which is really *Shānti* or Peace?

In the harbor and in the ocean there may be many different kinds of boats and ships. Big ships, as well as small ships, come into this harbor. There may be ships of great wonders that come into this harbor, and also ships from many different countries. These ships bring various kinds of things from many different places, and they also export various kinds of things from this country. Each ship that comes into this harbor may be a very subtle ship, and the things that are imported may also be very subtle. If the mind looks at these things it will say, "This is good, that is good. This brings peace, that is peace." This is what the mind will say, but after a very short time it will give these things away. Then it will say something else is good. The mind will become fascinated with something else, then it will give that thing away and say that something else is better. Then it will give that away and say something else is much nicer; again it will give that away and say something else is better than that. Within the next second the mind will bring something else. Within a second that kind of peace changes.

The kind of peace obtained from *māya* is like this, the state of peace for the body is like this, and that state of peace of mind is also like this. Because of this no one has lived in this world without desire, no one has lived here having completely annihilated his desires. There is no one who has bathed enough to get rid of all his dirt. There is no one who has rid himself of all the filth in his mind. There is no one who has completely satisfied his desires in this world. That state of peace of mind is like this. We are seeking to attain peace from something which has no peace. This mind is a thing which does not contain peace. This is something that we have to think about. We who are in search of peace of mind must understand what it is that should be made peaceful.

My children who are the gems of my eyes, there are many varieties of dogs. There are about one thousand, one hundred different varieties of dogs. These one thousand, one hundred different types of dogs may be many different colors. There may be many different things about these dogs. Although their colors, their hues, and their sounds may be different, their quality is that of a dog. It is a dog and it is always called a dog. Whether it is a tiny dog that can be put into your pocket, whether it is an Alsatian, or whether it is a dog that comes from Egypt or from some other place, it is still a dog. A dog is a dog.

You may train a dog to sleep on a bed, you may not feed it fish or meat, you may train it to stay in a dark room, you

169

may train it in any way, but that dog still has a natural instinct within it. You trained the dog to stay in a dark room where it did not see the sun or the moon, and then you say, "Okay, let's take this dog out for a ride and show it the world." When you bring it out into the world, that natural instinct of the dog is there—right away it starts to sniff everything. It keeps on looking for things, it goes on sniffing and smelling things out. That dog will go on sniffing and searching for filth, dirt, and feces. These are the things that the dog goes in search of. It will pull its leash in the direction of these things and will not come back without eating some feces. No matter how cleanly you might have brought up the dog, the moment you take it out of its enclosed room to show it the world, these are the things it goes in search of. This is the nature of the mind. Do not think that by holding onto this mind you can obtain peace. No matter how carefully you nurture and hold onto this mind, this is what it will do. You may nurture it very carefully in a place where there are so many colors, so many different kinds of things, and so many different forms, but you can never obtain peace of mind. Because for the dog feces are candy, to the dog feces are tasty—that is the nature of the dog. Evil things and dirty things are tasty to the dog.

All the things that are filthy in the world and all the things that have been discarded by God are what the mind likes. Whatever has been discarded from the Truth is what mind and desire like. That is what desire favors, and that is what the mind craves. It is only this smell that the mind knows. No matter how much you train it, this is what it will do. The mind will never give you peace. It will never give you peace at any time. Therefore, it is impossible to give peace to this mind even for one day.

In its natural state the mind has seven aspects of desire

in it. The mind is a dog, it is a monkey, it is a donkey, it is a tiger, it is a bull, it is a lion, it is a fox with many tricks. It is a snake, it is a donkey, it is a horse, it is a turtle, it is a hare, it is a lizard, it is a crocodile. Once a crocodile grabs something, it never lets it go. The mind is a pig, it is a rhinoceros. It is a large, graceful deer, and it is a very beautiful peacock. It is also a house of wonders and magic, it is a beautiful farm, it is a lovely flower garden, it is a fruit orchard. It is also total darkness that knows nothing, there is no light in that orchard. Therefore you cannot see anything, and you cannot pluck any fruits from this orchard. The mind has all of these different forms within it.

It is impossible to make this mind peaceful. We have to think—what is it that can be made peaceful? First of all, can we make the mind tranquil? It is impossible to tranquilize the mind. You can never make it peaceful even if you take a hundred and five million births, if you keep on dying and being reborn, dying and being reborn, dying and being reborn, even then that mind will never attain peace. Even if one is born over and over again, the mind will not attain peace. It is a hopeless concept to say that there is a state called peace of mind.

You have to understand what it is that has to be made peaceful and how it can be made peaceful. We need to search for Wisdom. The point is we need to understand how the Soul can attain Tranquility and Peace in the State of God. This Wisdom brings about Peace of the Soul. That Peace is with God and that is One Point. That State of Peace exists there. The Clarity of making the Soul Peaceful is there. We need to understand what has to be done in order to attain *Shānti*, Peace.

Māya has many different forms. This mind has many

different forms and many different qualities. Everyone is speaking about peace of mind, peace of mind—they talk of making the mind peaceful. Everyone talks about peace of mind in this way, but you can never make the mind peaceful. That is something that can never be done.

It is like the story of a king who brought up a cat. Having raised this cat, he then trained it, he trained it very well. The king used to read the *purānas* and the scriptures. He used to recite from the Bible, the scriptures, and the Qur'an. In those days there was no electric light. For that reason the king had trained the cat so that he could put a lamp on top of the cat's head and read by that light. So he kept the lamp on top of the cat's head. Whenever the oil lamp was placed on the cat's head the cat stayed in that one position. With the light of that lamp the king would read scriptures and books. He did this for many years.

One day as the king was doing this, he called his minister and asked, "Are habits and customs greater, or are inherited qualities greater?"

The minister said, "Heredity is greater."

Then the king said, "No, that's not correct, that is not the way it is. Habits and customs are greater." The king said to the minister, "If you do not give me a proper explanation of this within forty days, I will cut off your head." This is the order that he gave to the minister.

The minister thought, "What can I do? The king says that customs and habits are greater than inherited qualities. But if you bring up a horse, that horse will keep on neighing. This is the inherent quality of the horse. Can you ever stop that horse from neighing? You can train the horse, and you can ride on the horse, but you cannot stop it from neighing." Though the minister thought about this, he was still without a proper explanation for the king. He did not know what to do, and he did not know how to answer this question. The king insisted that he be given an answer, but it was not possible for the minister to give this explanation to the king or make him understand.

So the minister started thinking and investigating the matter. Then he saw the cat sitting with the lamp on its head. He asked, "Who could have placed the lamp on the cat's head?"

The king said, "I've raised this cat this way. I trained this cat this way, and for many years it has been keeping this lamp on its head. This is a habit it has learned. This quality is not something it has inherited. Therefore, habits are greater than inherited qualities."

Still the minister insisted, "No, heredity is greater."

Again the king threatened him and said, "If you cannot prove this within forty days, you will be killed."

The minister was very sad. He thought, "What can possibly be done?" He went to see his wife and asked her, "Will you be able to catch a mouse for me?"

The wife said, "All right. I'll catch a mouse for you."

Now it was the fortieth day, and this was a very crucial day. The minister took a small bag and placed the mouse inside it. He then placed the bag inside his sleeve. At this time all the kings had assembled there, since this was the day he was going to prove whether heredity was greater than habit. The king had called all the other kings together. He said, "Unless the minister proves that heredity is greater than habit, I am going to behead him today."

Then the minister said, "O great king, inherited qualities are greater than habits."

The king asked, "How can you prove this?" In order to prove this the minister let the mouse go while the cat was sitting there with the lamp on its head. At once the cat moved. By instinct, the cat immediately jumped on the mouse and caught it. The lamp fell from the cat's head and hit against the king's head. The kerosene in the lamp set fire to everything. Everyone ran around trying to help put out the fire.

The minister, pointing to the cat's actions, then said to the king, "Maharaja, see! This is what is meant by inherited qualities. By training the cat you created certain habitual qualities. But this is its inherent quality, this is the quality that is inherent within this cat. This is its inherited quality, and this is the quality that is within it. No one can change this quality. Even though you trained this cat to keep this lamp on its head, even though you trained it to sit still, it is impossible for you to stop it from behaving according to its inherent qualities."

As a result of the fire, the king's hair had been burned, and everything had been damaged. The whole place was in a state of disorder.

The quality of the mind is like this. It is like the inherited qualities. The five elements of earth, fire, water, air, and space are the qualities of the body which are formed within the mind. These seven qualities of earth, fire, water, air, space, mind, and desire are the seven *nāfs* [evil desires] found within the body. No matter how much you train the mind, if it sees something which attracts it, immediately it will jump. As soon as it sees food it will jump. As soon as it sees its intention it will jump. These are the inherited qualities of the mind. Therefore, do not think that you can ever train this mind. It is impossible to do this! The quality that is inherent within the mind will never attain peace. There is no place to bring about stillness or peace of mind. As long as the world exists, the mind can never be made peaceful. As long as there is illusion, the mind cannot be made peaceful. As long as there are glitters, the mind cannot be made peaceful. Therefore, we have to know what it is that will give us Peace.

The mind will sit quietly, it will wait and be very quiet, then it will seize its victim. It will be very quiet like the cat. Among all animals, you will find that the cat family is very quiet. When they walk, you do not hear any noise from them. You can hear the sounds of even a rat running. But the mind is like the cat—it moves very silently without anybody noticing it. It goes in such a very subtle manner, and then it seizes its object. When the mind takes the form of the cat it thinks, "The entire world is contained within me. So if I close my eyes everything will become dark. When I close my eyes the entire world becomes dark. Since the whole world is contained within me, the world comes into being only when I open my eyes. When I close my eyes, the world disappears." When the mind takes the form of the cat, this is what it thinks.

In this manner the mind goes in search of its prey. It creeps into the kitchen very quietly. It closes its eyes and begins lapping the milk. What does it think at this time? It thinks, "I have closed my eyes, therefore no one sees me now. No one can see me because I have closed my eyes." It continues drinking the milk. But suddenly the cook comes and sees the cat drinking the milk. The cook beats the cat who cries "Meow!" and runs away. But its intention to steal this milk remains the same, so it comes back again. The mind again takes the form of a cat and comes back to drink the milk. It believes that if it closes its eyes the world no longer exists. In the same way, whatever takes the form of the cat will act this way.

When the mind takes the form of a bull, it thinks: "I am the one who is carrying the world, and I am also protecting the world. I am the one who plows. I am the one who carries these loads. I take loads back and forth to the house. I carry these loads on my back and pull these carts. Who else will bring this cart from the farm to the house? Other than me no one else knows how to farm. It is I who take care of the husband. I protect the wife and children. It is I who do the farming and plowing of the fields. It is I who supply the family with food." This is what the bull thinks.

When the mind takes the form of a bull, it thinks, "If not for me, nothing would happen. No one else would supply food, only I can supply food." But if you put two extra loads on its back, it groans and bellows because it cannot pull the cart and the load. In the same way when sorrow afflicts the mind, the mind cannot carry that even for one second. If you are sick and have diarrhea just twice, you become very weak. When you have diarrhea you are finished. Then the mind says, "Aah! Oh! There is no one here to carry me!" This is the way the mind works.

If the mind becomes a tiger, it keeps its eyes focused on its prey. When the mind takes the form of a tiger, if it sees something it folds itself up and stares very hard at its object. It looks at its prey and then starts moving its tail. Having moved its tail for awhile, immediately it jumps on its prey. Like this, the mind has kept within it a form for each and every thing.

Sometimes the mind bends its head down and acts like a snake. Some snakes have a rattle that makes a vibrating sound. Another kind of snake just lies still with its head down waiting for its prey. When it sees something, it immediately attacks and seizes it. There is also the cobra. As soon as somebody passes by, it warns him by raising its hood and hissing. It says, "I am here. Do not come near me. I am not going to harm you, and you must not harm me." When Wisdom comes, the mind takes the form of a snake. The snake has no vision, and that is why it raises its hood and hisses. In the same way, the qualities of the mind and the forms of the mind are indescribable. Yet we think it is possible to make the mind peaceful and tranquil. It is impossible to do this.

We have to find out what its connections are, we need to understand the connections of the mind. The mind has within it a powerful magnet. It has many, many forces within it. The mind has four hundred trillion, ten thousand *saktis* or forces within it. God has said that the mind is a secret. The mind is a very big secret. Within that secret is the *Zāt* and the *sifat*. The *Zāt* is His Grace and *sifat* is all of creation. All these creations are within the mind. There is a big ocean within the mind of man, there is a big ocean of *māya* within the mind. There is also an Ocean of Knowledge within the mind. That Endless Plenitude of God is also within it. This is the mind. Until we understand through which process it is possible to bring peace to the mind, it will be very difficult to attain *Shānti*. In fact, you can never make the mind peaceful.

Before one is able to have *Shānti*, one will have *vānti* [nausea]. All the food that is eaten will be *vānti*. When Wisdom comes, all the things the mind relishes and loves are *vanti* to him. As soon as one starts on the journey to find Peace of the Soul, every aspect of the mind that he sees and everything the mind captures is nauseating to him. Every form is *vānti* to him. All the things the mind takes and eats are *vānti* to him. As Wisdom begins to grow and grow, everything the mind takes is *vānti* to him. It is not *Shānti*, it is *vānti*. When the connection of *Imān* and Wisdom comes, everything the mind touches is *vānti* to him. Do not think that this is Peace.

Peace of the Soul is real Peace. This is True Peace and this is within God. This is the State of His *Zāt* which is within the *Qalb*, and this is known as the *'Arsh ul-Mū'min*. It is called the Throne of God and it is within the Kingdom of God. This is the State in which God exists, and it is this that is called *Shānti*. Peace of the Soul is real Peace.

We think that the section of God is very, very difficult, but it is very easy. This is very easy to attain. It is very easy because you can see an end to it. Within this history an end can be seen. Because of this, it is very easy to attain Peace of the Soul in the Kingdom of God. We can attain Peace of the Soul. But it is impossible to make this mind peaceful because it has so many endless forces of illusion within it.

The mind thinks like the cat and the bull. The bull thinks, "I must become like this. I must make myself into this. I must do this. I must do that." As a result of this, many sorrows and sufferings may follow. It is because of this that these monkeys are born. These monkeys will destroy everything that has been built up. The mind exists in the state of the monkey, the bull, and the goat.

It is not at all possible to bring peace to the mind. This is why the mind is called a monkey. A common term for the mind is 'monkey' or the 'monkey mind'. In Tamil *purānas*, instead of illustrating it as a monkey mind, they make a comparison and call it *Anjanadēvi*. *Anjanadēvi* emerged from the five sections. *Anjanēhan's* mother is *Anjanadēvi*. *Anjanadēvi* is the five elements: earth, fire, water, air, and space. The mind was born from the section of these five elements—the mind came out of this one fistful of earth. They call that a god and make illustrations of it as a god. *Anjanēhan* is the son of *Anjanadēvi*, that is, the friend of the five elements; the friend of these five elements is the monkey mind. Who is the father of these five elements? It is said in the *purānas* that *Vāyubagavān* [air] is the father of the five elements. *Ānjanadēvi* and *Vāyubagavān* came together and gave birth to the monkey mind. The monkey mind is called *Ānjanēhan*, and it is also known as *Hanumān*.

This mind never dies, it will never die. As long as these five elements of earth, fire, water, air, and space exist, the mind will exist. As long as these five elements exist, the mind will also exist. Therefore, my children, you must think. Children, gems of my eyes, it is not possible to make the mind peaceful. The mind cannot be killed, nor can it be made peaceful. You have to reflect and search for a way in which these connections can be cut away.

It is very difficult to control the mind. This mind is like a *gekko* [wall lizard]. It can move horizontally or vertically. The *gekko* has only one level of consciousness. Some people think that the sounds of the *gekko* predict horoscopes. But the *gekko* has only one level of consciousness: one quarter of its consciousness is spent looking for prey, one quarter is spent watching where it is going, one quarter is spent on preventing itself from being captured by other animals, and one quarter of its consciousness is spent making sounds. Still it has only one kind of consciousness. The mind is like that because it has only one point, it has only the point of illusion. This very dark wisdom is all that the mind has.

The *gekko* spends only one quarter of its consciousness making sounds. But when man, who has the sixth level of consciousness [Divine Analytic Wisdom] hears the sound of the *gekko*, he says, "There is some danger ahead of us. There is danger over there. Some danger will come to us." Man loses his sixth level of consciousness and descends to a state in which he has less than half the consciousness of a *gekko*. Man, who has six levels of consciousness, descends to a state in which he has even less than half a level of

179

consciousness—he does not have even a quarter of that consciousness; he has about one-eighth consciousness. Man has the potential to know what is right and wrong, but now he has become a victim of the sounds of the *gekko*.

The point or aim of the *gekko* is to catch every insect and eat it. It will catch all the beetles, flies, and insects. There is a kind of magnet within it—in each of its four legs there is a certain kind of suction magnet which grabs and holds onto the elements. It attaches itself onto the roof or onto the wall. It can go upward, and it can come downward. It can go up again vertically, and it can run horizontally. The wall lizard has this kind of magnetic attraction within it. It has a magnetic attraction to the wall in its tail, and that magnet is also there in its legs. When it puts its tongue out, it can catch its prey because it also has a magnetic substance in its tongue. Even in its thought there is that magnet.

The mind, which has one level of consciousness, forgets the fact that at some time the angel of death is going to catch it. It forgets that the Truth will come and destroy it. It forgets all of this. Like the *gekko* the mind will advise others, but it will never advise itself. Since it has this magnetic force within it, if there is a connection to the earth, the mind will go in that direction. If it has a connection to air, then it will go to the air. If the mind has a connection to fire, it will go to the fire. If it has a connection to creation, the mind will go towards creation. If it has the differences of races and religions, the mind will go in that direction. If it has a connection to the mind, then it will go there. If it has a connection to desire, it will go in the direction of desire.

So like that, the mind will go up and down. The mind will keep on rotating up and down. Each time, it is going to catch its prey. This is the connection that the mind has. This is the aspect of the mind. It will always be in a state of movement, moving up and down. If one of these connections is there, the magnet of the mind will cling to that connection. It will never die. This is why you can never attain peace of mind. You can never tranquilize or make the mind peaceful. It cannot be killed either.

Therefore, how can we win over the mind? My children who are the gems of my eyes, all these channels and connections that are within the mind must be severed. This section which relates to the earth must be severed. If there is no connection to earth, then the mind cannot hold onto that. If there is no connection to fire, the mind cannot hold onto that. If you sever the connection to water, then the mind cannot cling to that. If the section of air is severed, then the mind cannot hold onto that. If the section of ether is severed, then the mind cannot hold onto that. If you cut off the connection of the monkey mind and cut off the connection of desire, then it cannot hold onto those. The mind will just fall flat because it has nothing that it can hold onto, it has nothing to which it can cling. It no longer has the thing to which it is attracted. Whenever it tries to cling to something, it will just fall because it cannot run in all directions. It cannot run vertically or horizontally. It cannot go through the anal fire, it cannot go through creation or seminal fluids, it cannot go into the body because there is no support for it. The mind will fall.

If you can cut off all of the supports for the mind, it will have no support and it will have to fall down. Once it falls, it will keep on moving within itself, and at that time you can capture it and tie it with a strong rope. Then put the mirror of Wisdom in front of it so that it can look at itself. It will look at itself and will grieve over its state, and finally it will die. Then we can continue to do our work.

It is like this. Without approaching the mind in this way,

if we say that we can kill the mind, that we can make the mind peaceful, or that we can win over the mind, we can never do it. As long as the mind. has a connection to the world, it will exist. Through Wisdom the connections of the mind must be severed. If you can sever these connections through Wisdom, then you will attain Peace of the Soul. That is real Peace. Freedom of the Soul is real Peace.

The two different sections of peace must be understood. One is called peace of mind, and one is Peace of the Soul. Peace of the Soul is easy to attain. To obtain peace of mind is very difficult because the mind has no end—the mind has no end. You think that it is very easy to make the mind peaceful, but it is not easy. It is difficult because when one form goes, another form comes. One form goes and another form comes. Therefore, the mind can never be peaceful; it can never give you peace. It is the other state, Peace of the Soul, that can be reached. This is True Peace. Therefore, my children, you must think about this, you must reflect on this.

To understand this Peace, you need Faith. Search for and obtain that Faith. In that State, search for Divine Wisdom and God's Divine Qualities. For some, when those Qualities, that Wisdom, and that State are realized, it is milk to the *Qalb*, for others it is like honey, to some it is like a fruit, for some it is like *kastūri*, for some it is like *ghee*, for some it is a taste, for some it is very beautiful, for some it is like a flower garden, for some it is heaven, for some it is bliss, for some it is a fragrance. For some it is a state of no suffering, a state of bliss, the state of a sixteen year old. For some it is paradise. For some it is Light, for some it is *Gnānam* [Wisdom], for some it is the Radiance of Wisdom, for some it is the world of the Soul. For some it is a mirror, for some it is like a television, for some it is like a radio. For some it is God. It is the Light of God. To some it is Plenitude.

Like this, according to the intentions of your search, it will reveal that State and that Bliss to you in many ways. It is this Fragrance, this *Qalb*, that can bestow *Shānti*. Only that Creator, that *Rabb*, can give you *Shānti*. That is the Place where Undiminishing Grace exists resonating *Allāhu*.

If you can find out what it is that you really need, and if you obtain that State of Peace, that is the Real State of Peace. In that State everything you ask for will be given. That is the State of *Firdaus*, the highest and most blissful heaven. It is the Tree *Sidratul Muntaha*, which bears the Fruit of Grace. That Place from which Peace can be obtained must be understood.

The section of Peace of the Soul and the section of peace of mind must be understood. These two aspects must be understood. That point must be understood. We must realize what it is that can be in that State of Peace. In order to understand this you need Wisdom. Please reflect on this, my children, please think about this. *Ameen*.

May God protect us and sustain us. May He give us His State of Peace. *Ameen*. *Ya Rabbil'ālameen*. O Ruler of the universes, may this intention be fulfilled.

May He protect us. *Ameen*. May He always show us the Straight Path, open that State of Peace for us, and feed us with His Honey of Grace. *Ameen*.

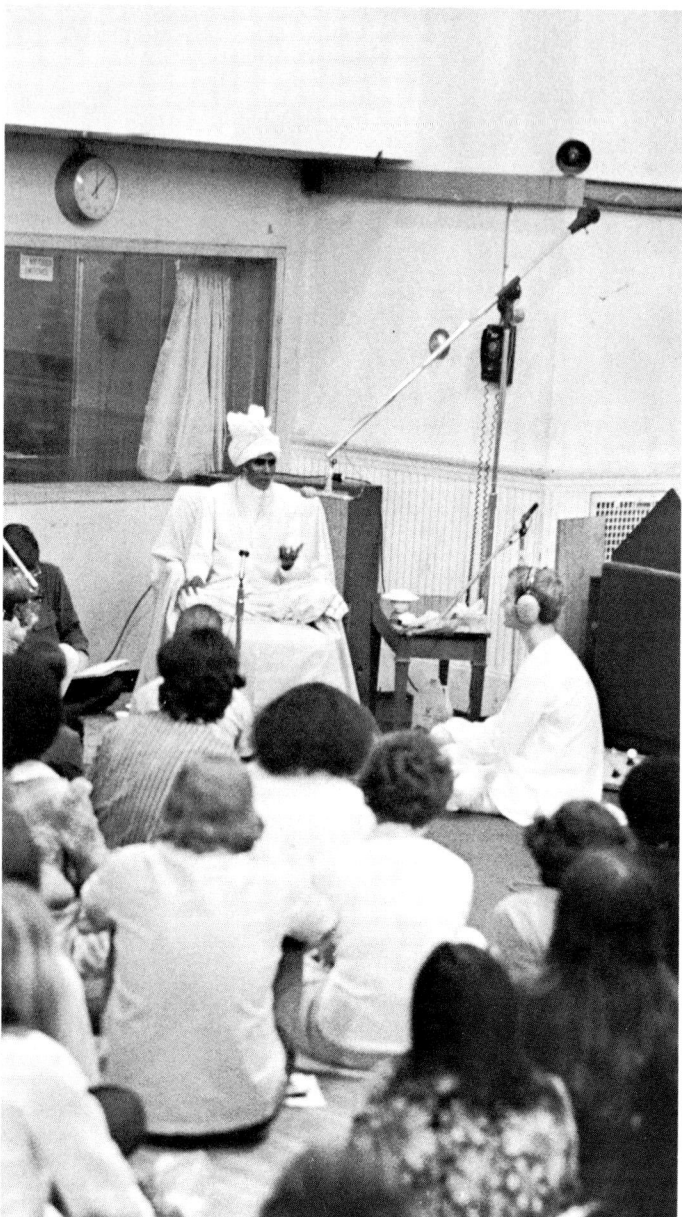

Beyond Form

Radio interviewer Lex Hixon has frequently invited His Holiness Bawa Muhaiyaddeen to appear on the Sunday morning "In the Spirit" program on WBAI-FM, New York.

The subject matter of these interviews has ranged from questions on meditation, yoga, and other spiritual practices to very serious and in-depth discussions of the essential nature of God, the real purpose of human life, and reasons for the apparent existence of the world. Several of these interviews are collected in a small book entitled Truth and Light: brief explanations.

The interview printed here took place on November 16, 1975, at the WBAI studios in New York City. Bawa describes True Peace as the experience of being without form, of knowing God as the formlessness of the Human Soul, as the quality of Infinite Compassion for all lives.

185

LEX HIXON

First, would Bawa speak about this Guru which is *Allāh,* which is the Ultimate Guru? Secondly, can ordinary people experience this ultimate Guru, or is it just for special advanced souls that have evolved very high? The third aspect would be: what about the apparent human form of the Guru? That is obviously something that is just projected out there provisionally. How will that disappear?

BAWA

Children, who are the gems within my eyes, children who are the compassionate ones within my heart and within my love, I extend greetings to the children who are here, as well as to all the children who are listening to the radio broadcast. I extend the greetings of a small one. If there are any faults, please forgive me. I am an unlettered person. I am a very tiny person. If there are any faults, please forgive me. My greetings.

My children, who are the light of my eyes, and who are the fruits of my heart, I convey my loving greetings to you. To the question asked by a most precious child—God is a Power. God transcends all forces and energies. A cell could be subdivided into millions and millions of different types of cells. Blood is a cell. A form is also a cell. The air is a cell. The water is a cell. The fire is a cell. The light that comes from our eyes is a cell. The mind is a cell. The ether is also a cell. Like that, there are millions and millions and millions of cells.

There is a Treasure which creates these cells. *Māya* [illusion] is a cell, earth is a cell, satan is a cell, darkness is a cell, desire is a cell, and mind is a cell. Like this, cells are created. The Power which controls all these cells after creating them is God. This Power is like a Form within the form. That which is the Form within the form is something we have to analyze. That Form cannot be seen by everyone. The mind, therefore, cannot comprehend it. Mind and desire are searching for this thing which has given them awareness. Even the cells are searching for this Reality. Every creation is searching for this Power. The oceans, the lands, the skies, the nether worlds, all lives, atoms, everything is searching for this Power. They are all in search of this Power, but this Power exists where it exists. This Power has no form, no shape, no color, no race, no religion. This Power has no story, no color, no wife or children, no kingdom, and no place. Because this Power has no story, the mind thinks about it.

Of all the forms that the mind creates, none of them can move. You can draw a picture with the mind, or you may practice psychology; but whatever you create with the mind will not move. All the things you may create will not move. They will only stay in the place where they have been put. If you draw a flower, there is no fragrance in that flower, there is no movement in that flower. If you draw a tree, it does not move, the fruit does not move or grow. None of these things happen there. But there are certain things that keep on moving. The mind wonders and asks, "Where is the thing that causes movement?" The mind claims, "I am God." Desire says, "I am God. I am the one who is ruling this world." The body says, "There is nothing greater than I." Mind and desire create all these creations and say, "I am God." But none of these creations have life or movement. They may be in the form of art or in the form of sculpture, but they do not move.

There is a Power which moves these creations. It is that Power which keeps these things moving. The mind and desire, therefore, begin to reflect about that Power.

Man's story thinks about it, his thought thinks about it, and his learning thinks about it. They think, "There is some Treasure somewhere. There is some Treasure that keeps everything moving."

The mind says: "I have done all this, but it does not speak. So there must be a power, coming from somewhere, which causes movement and speech. Can that be God? Where is that God? Is it within earth, fire, water, air, or space? I have made a form out of these five elements. God must exist within these five. It is within these five that this power moves. I created this form," says the mind, "but there must be some other force which moves it. Maybe that is God." The mind thus begins to think about what God is.

The mind creates a dog and asks, "Is God like that?" Then it creates a snake and asks, "Is God like that?" Then it creates a bull, asking if God is like that. The mind sees everything outside, makes a thought form out of it, and retains that within itself. It makes a crow, a dog, a donkey, a goat, a horse, a snake, a scorpion, an elephant, a peacock, a crow, and a cock. Like this, the mind creates four hundred trillion, ten thousand such things and watches them. It makes three hundred and thirty million gods. It makes forty-eight thousand *rishis* [spiritual teachings]. It creates satan and illusion. It creates everything, but those things just stay where they are. There is no movement or growth within them. Then the mind thinks, "I have created these things, but they remain where they are."

Then it begins to worship them, saying, "*Om, Sakti, Sivam, Radhā, Gopāla, Krishna, Hare Rama.*" The mind says, "Now I have given these creations names; I have called them *Sakti* and *Sivam*, but even after I have given

188

names to these creations, sang songs and praises to them, read their horoscopes, and recited the *panjācharam* [the five-lettered *mantra*], they still do not move."

Then the mind thinks, "Surely there must be some other power, somewhere, that makes these creations move." Thus the mind goes in search of God. After it creates all these forms, recites *mantras*, and does so many things, still none of these things move.

All these forms are now found inside the mind. That Power is within. That Power alone is God. All these things that have been done may be described as *saktis* [forces or energies]. These *saktis* are what God does *not* have within Him. He does not have this story within Him. God took this story out, kept it outside of Himself, and became weightless. He remained as Pure Light, as Power. It is that Power which we call God. That Power is within that form, it is within that point. It is an atomless thing. It has no form. It has no story.

The *gnānis*, the *swamis*, the *purānas*, and the religions, however, sang songs and made praises to the forms that the mind created. What was created by the mind was made into a form and kept there. The mind said, "Oh, my father, save me!" It created a snake, it made a form of the snake, and said, "Oh, my father, protect me!" Then it created the elephant. But what does the elephant have? It has arrogance. It created the peacock and worshipped it. But what does the peacock have? It has five colors. Then the mind created a crow and worshipped that. But what do crows have? They have black color. Then it created a dog and worshipped that. What does the dog have? The dog has desire. Like this, the mind created many different forms.

There is One Point. That Point is formless. That Point is a Power. That Power exists within each and every life, including the tiniest infant. To realize that Power we need a television camera, and we also need a telephone. You must take away all the forms that the mind has created and put them outside. Take them and discard them. Once you have taken all the forms that the mind has created and placed them outside, then you need Wisdom to look at that Power. We must begin to research and understand, while holding the magnet which is Wisdom. Within this magnet is that Light-Power. As you keep on moving the magnet of Wisdom, the Power of God will draw it. In the same way that iron is pulled by a magnet, these seven levels of Wisdom—perception, awareness, intellect, judgment, Wisdom, Divine Analytic Wisdom, and Divine Luminous Wisdom—get pulled into that Power. As soon as this magnet touches that Power, it gets drawn into it with a lot of force. As soon as the Power takes it in, we will see our Father.

None of the forms that we saw earlier exist within our Father. What you will see there is that All-Pervading, Powerful Light. There will be no form in that Light. When you look further into that Power, it will be in the Form of Compassionate Love. When you look still further, you will find Tolerance and Peacefulness. You will find that Point existing within everyone. It exists as Perfect Peace everywhere. Doing duty without any selfishness, that Point shows Love and Compassion to everyone. It performs duty without any selfishness. That Point carries everybody and feeds them with the Milk of Grace. It embraces, it gives Peace, it teaches Good Qualities, it shows Patience.

That Point shows rare and precious Qualities. It shows Patience within, it shows Contentment and Surrender. It becomes the Slave to the slave. It is the Love intermingled within love. It is this which is merged within us.

As soon as that Divine Wisdom comes within us, these forms will leave us. All the forms that we have created, and all the worship that we have done will leave us. All that we have seen will disappear. What we see beyond that is the Grace of God, that Power. That is what is called Grace. That is what is called Divine Wisdom. When we look with His Grace, what we see is His Divine Power. What is that Power? It is His Divine Qualities, His Divine Actions, His Divine Love, His Divine Compassion, His Divine Justice, His Inner Patience, His Tolerance, and His Peacefulness. That Power is His Quality of loving all lives as His own life, His Quality of treating all distresses as His own distress, His Quality of treating all hunger as His own hunger, and His Quality of treating all illnesses as His own illness. It is that State of Peace and that State of Tranquility. We must see that State which is God. God is everywhere. He exists in everything. What we have to search for is Divine Wisdom.

When *Khidhr Nabi* [the Eternal Prophet] found that Divine Wisdom, he immediately saw that Formless Form. When you search for that Wisdom and find it, what is now inside you will be revealed to you outside. Your form disappears and the Formless State comes out. Everybody can attain that, everybody can reach that State. Everybody can reach that State. Everybody can reach God. The man who possesses Divine Analytic Wisdom can reach that. What do we need in order to reach that? Once Divine Wisdom dawns in us, we can reach our Father. His Grace is found in each one, from the infant to everyone else.

God has created a farm in which He has placed those crops, but unfortunately, weeds have grown. The weeds of illusion have grown. These weeds are also found naturally. Darkness has also grown. Insects and worms have come to the farm, and they are destroying the good crops. They have covered the good crops, and they are destroying them. We have to remove the weeds. We must remove these weeds. If we spray those weeds with a chemical that can kill them, those weeds will die. Then the Truth will emerge. If we do this, then that Truth will emerge. If we can pluck all those weeds with our Wisdom, then that Power which is within us will emerge. That is God. That is that Power. That is what is called *Āndevan* [God]. It is found in every heart, and it is this that we have to understand. All of us can reach it, but we must imbibe the Qualities of God and reach that Divine Wisdom. The Form of God exists in that State. We have to put away everything that the mind has created. The things that the mind creates will not move, and they will not carry us. We can never see this Power with those *saktis* or forces. They are just *saktis* which are called *rishis*.

Because God has no form, His Slaves and *Gnānis* [Divinely Wise Ones] could not show Him to the people who questioned them. When people asked them, "Where is God?" and "Who is God?" the Slaves and *Gnānis* of God had to escape.

Therefore they said, "God is like an effulgence," and they showed a fire. They said, "God is like a resplendence," and they showed the sun. They said, "This is how God is. He is like this." They had to show an example in order to escape. When they said, "He has the coolness of the moon," the people asked, "How will that coolness be?" So the *Gnānis* and *Swamis* showed the moon as an example. Then they said, "God is like a star," and they showed them a star as an example. Then they said, "He is everywhere," and showed another object for that. Because the *Gnānis* could not take God and show Him to the people, they had to try to show God through different forms and examples. But this is not God. This form is not His Form. This is not That. Once this form is destroyed and we go beyond, we have to give up that outside form. We have to go beyond the form! Then we meet that Power. If we understand this, we can reach God. Everyone can do this, it is found within everyone. You do not have to go outside in search of this. My children, who are the gems of my eyes, it is very easy.

That answers two of your questions, now to answer the third question.

When that Divine Wisdom comes into you, this form will have already left you. The Magnet of your Wisdom will now repel everything that the mind has created, and the Divine Wisdom will be drawn by that Divine Power. You must search for that Magnet which is Wisdom. Please search for that.

The mind, which somersaults all over, must be controlled and kept in prison. These five elements which somersault must be imprisoned. The earth has many *saktis*. The fire has many *saktis*, the air has many *saktis*. There is *Pārvadi* and *Pāramēsvari*. *Pār* means earth. There is *Pāramēsvari*, which is the *sakti* of the earth. When you say fire, it is *Akkinibagavān*, which is synonymous with the angel of death. There is the angel Michael, or *Varunabagavān*, who is the angel of water. *Vāyubagavān* is the angel of air, *Īsrafīl*. *Pārvadi* and *Pāramēsvari* are Adam and Eve. *Pār* means the earth. *Pāramēsvari* means that the earth is spread all over. Then there is *āhāyam* which means ether or space, and it is also called *māya* or the mind. These are the five elements. These five elements are now being depicted as God. Those things that the five elements have created are what is called the mind or illusion. These five are also called the five elements or the five celestial angels. This we must think about. Once we start reflecting on this, we realize that these are not God, they are merely angels. These angels cannot give us heaven. We have to think about this. My children, who are the gems within my eyes, you must please think about this. You must reflect over it. That which we see as a form will automatically disappear.

In the story of *Khidhr Nabi,* God said, "All that you saw up until now is what the mind showed you. All the *gurus* that you have seen were just forms. Look at Gabriel. What you saw earlier was just the forms of the mind, but you did not see Me. Now look at Me." Then Gabriel turned into a Light, he was neither male nor female. God told *Khidhr Nabi:* "All this time your mind saw the form of Gabriel as a man. It was this form that you were worshipping, this form was in your desire, it was the form that you saw with your eyes. This was what your physical eyes saw, what your intellect saw, what your actions saw, and this form was what you were seeing all this time. Now look at Me." God said, "When you look at Me, you see Me as a form. This is the form of God that the mind created. This is the form of God that you had in your mind. This is what you saw. Look at Gabriel now. He has turned into Light, he is neither male nor female, he has neither form nor formlessness. This is that State. All the time that you have been walking with him and learning with him, it was just a form that your mind desired. Now look at Me." God said, "I am an Effulgence. I am a Radiance. Before this you saw Me and spoke to Me, but this was only the form of your mind. Now look at Me. Am I in a state of form? No. I am beyond form. This is what I am. The one who sees Me will never go wrong."

This is what God told Moses: "If anyone sees Me once, he will not commit any faults in the world. He will be merged within Me. He is Me and I am him." Then there is no world in him, there is no suffering in him, there is no happiness in him, there is no business in him. There is no *ah-eee* in him, *ah-ing* does not exist.

"He speaks to Me and I speak to him," God says. "It is this Communion which exists. These Sounds are what exist. My Prince listens to Me, and I listen to his words." This is the State of Unity. Other than that, this *ah-ing, kuing* is nothing. There is no business at all in this Unity. There is no *om* business. There are no differences in that State. That is that Point.

God said: *"Khidhr*, look! Now can you see Me? This is that Point. Please understand this. If you understand this Point, I am that Power. Please reflect over that. Please understand that." This is what God explained to *Khidhr*. In that State, *Khidhr* was formless. When *Khidhr* merged into That, God said, "You are Me and I am you. Now do you duty. Go and do your duty."

If we have to travel somewhere, we have a ship. If we want to fly somewhere, we have a plane. If we want to understand anything, a microscope is there. If we want to see the entire universe, a television is within us. If we want to see what is right and wrong, we have a scale in our hands. If we want to see what is within and what is without, we have a television camera. We have all of these instruments within us, but we need a Father to show us which instrument to take and which instrument to use.

A *guru* cannot show us that because *guru* means

business. *Guru-mantras* are always business *mantras*. The *guru* and disciple become similar to business associates. That is a broker association. You have a hundred brokers and one teacher. You receive half the profits and the teacher receives half the profits. It is like the fruits of an apple tree, half to you and half to the business broker. The one who plucks the apples gets ten percent, the person who owns the shop gets ten percent, the one who owns the apples gets ten percent, the person who owns the truck gets ten percent, and the driver gets five percent. Once it goes to the cooperative store, the owner of the store also gets a certain percentage. Finally, you pay forty-five cents for an apple. Actually, one hundred apples cost only one dollar. But by the time these profits are distributed in all those different ways, it becomes forty-five cents for one apple. This is what business means.

This is not like that. You have to pluck your own apple and taste the sweetness of that apple. There is no need for any *guru* business there. That is only good for all the things the mind has created. Legal work and broker work both come under what the mind has created.

Two days ago, one of the children here was on a bus. There were three people talking on the bus. This child overheard the conversation.

A man said, "I have a *mantra*, and I have joined a certain organization. As a result of joining, I receive so much value from it. A lot of peace comes out of it, and I get a lot of money. I have a lot of peace."

One of the girls in the party asked, "What is this peace that you are talking about?"

The man said, "There is plenty of happiness in it."

Then the girl asked, "What is the price for it?"

He said, "Two hundred dollars. If a person pays two

hundred dollars, then he will get grace. You also can get grace."

Then the girl said, "So if I give two hundred dollars, will I get all this peace and happiness?"

Then the other girl said, "You don't have to pay two hundred dollars. If you give me fifty dollars, I will disclose the *mantra* to you."

One of the children here overheard this conversation. That girl on the bus said, "Pay fifty dollars and you can have this *guru-mantra*." Now what can we do about this? We have to think about this. This is what is called business. This is a very good business. Please do not go in search of this.

You must understand the Father who is within you. The Treasure is within you. What do you need? You need Divine Wisdom. What do you need to achieve? Peace of mind. Please try to develop the Qualities of Compassion and Love.

The form of illusion is merely one fistful of earth. It is like the water saying, "If I go towards the fire, I will reach peace." Or it is like the fire saying, "If I go towards the water, I will reach peace of mind." The firewood thought, "If I go closer to the fire, I will reach that state of peace." So the firewood went toward the fire to reach peace. As it got closer to the fire, the fire began to consume the firewood. The wood said, "I am having peace, peace..." Finally, all the firewood was burned to ashes.

All of you are going in search of peace of mind now. Where are you going? You say *ahhhhhh-ing*. You are going back to baby talk. When you were babies trying to crawl on your belly, you used these same words, *ahhhhhh-ing, riiiinnnng, oonnnng*. This is the language of infants. You are now repeating those same words and trying to reach peace. You say *riiinnng*. You ask little children, "Do you want *oonga?"* meaning, "Do you want milk?" Then they say, *"oonng."* I have heard children saying this. I have heard infants saying this. Now you are saying this and trying to reach peace. This is the greatest wonder. It is like giving your mind to illusion. It will completely destroy your existence. This is not the thing that will produce peace.

If you pour water onto fire, the fire will be extinguished. If you bring fire towards water, the water will evaporate. If you put firewood in fire, the firewood becomes ashes. This is not peace. We have to think about this. We have to use Wisdom. We are men, we are human beings. We must try to understand what can produce peace of mind.

The mind is a demon, the mind is a dog, the mind is a monkey, the mind is a donkey, the mind is a bull, the mind is a lion, the mind is a tiger, the mind is a wolf, the mind is a hyena, the mind is a snake, the mind is an elephant, the mind is a rhinoceros. The mind has so many dangerous qualities in it. It is a demon, it is illusion, it is a worm. The mind is a stage with dancers on it. The mind is a football. It is playing tennis. The mind is a ghost. It is a baby. The mind is also crazy; the mind is a very crazy thing. This mind has so many duties to perform. This is what the mind is.

How can you bring about peace of mind by saying *ah-ing?* You can never, never produce peace this way. You are saying these words in a state of torpor. You can never bring peace to your Wisdom with those words. While you are saying *ah-ing* the price of gasoline has gone up. What is happening is that your money is wasting away. Food prices have gone up. There are more heavy rains today. There are hurricanes and gales that come and destroy us. They are also destroying all the farm products. There are new and dangerous types of diseases. New types of cancerous diseases are coming. Reciting these *mantras* ultimately destroys the entire population.

You have forgotten what Wisdom is. You have forgotten God. You have forgotten *Shanti,* or True Peace. You are saying *om, ah-ing, ring,* you are reciting these things. You can never reach peace by this. It is the same as the firewood trying to find peace in the fire, or like the water trying to find peace in the fire. It is like a cock bird going to the lion to find peace. It is very easy to reach that kind of peace. The majority of people are trying to reach this kind of peace, and many have achieved this kind of peace. But you are human beings, you have Wisdom. Please think about this carefully. Please, each of you, think of this. Think about this with your conscience. Think within yourself. When you say *ah-ing,* do you really reach peace, or does your mind go roaming around the world looking here and there? How can your mind achieve peace in this way? You have to think of this. Your Wisdom has to think about this.

Children, gems of my eyes, you should not get angry for what I have to say. I am only doing my duty. One who has no Wisdom is saying this. This is what you have to reflect upon. Do not hold onto something and say that it is correct. Please think about what I have to say. Please reflect on what I am saying. Take it, bite it, chew it, and see what this tastes like. Taste this as much as you tasted that other thing.

For business that thing might be alright. That business will grow very fast. For praise it is alright, but that praise will be destroyed one day. For that kind of peace it is alright, but very soon that might lead to cancer. Therefore, my children, please think.

To reach the Peace of God you must realize Wisdom and then reach the State that is called Peace. Please think about this. Reflect upon it. Please think with Wisdom and find out what *Shānti*—Peace—really means.

All this time you have been using your mind to find peace. You are holding onto that kind of peace. There is some peace for the brokers who do this. But if you really and truly think about it in your own heart, you will find that while you are saying these words your mind has gone to some business, or to a guest house, or to a rest house, or to play tennis. This is how the mind keeps on revolving, but that is not peace. What happens as a result of that is nausea. Finally, we are left with nausea. If you really reflect over that with your mind, you will realize the truth.

You should not get angry with what I say. The profits and losses are entirely yours. I do not get any profits out of this. But because I came, it is my duty to say what has to be said. Please think, please reflect over it. Whatever you think is a good income, do that. But this is not the way to tranquilize the mind. This will tranquilize your mind at one time, and the next time it will produce nausea.

The baby will cry for something, and if you buy that thing and give it to the baby, it will smile. The next minute it will look at another thing in the shop and say, "I want that." It will start crying. Then you will have to buy that. The next moment it will drop that and ask for another toy, and then you have to buy that. Then it wants a beer, and you have to buy a beer for it. That *shānti* or peace lasts just a few minutes. The mind will go on asking for everying that is found in the shop, and you have to go on feeding it. Do you think this is peace of mind?

The mind has taken several millions of forms and several millions of forces. The mind creates magic and colors. But you must control the mind in order to bring it peace. This may be what your experience is, this may be what your faith is, this may be what your understanding is. But what you are holding, please, put it down for awhile. With Wisdom reflect upon God.

There is a Power within you which controls everything. That is the Power which will subdue the mind and cut away the currents of *māya* which are connected to the mind. It will cut away all the magnetism within the mind. It will cut away all the forces of the earth, it will cut away the forces of the air, and it will cut away all the forces. That Power is that which will create Peace.

My children, who are the gems within my eyes, please think. I am not trying to force you into this. You should not get angry. Do not scold me. In the same way that each one comes and says something, I too am saying something. Then I will go away. You can do it the way you like. If you like this, do it this way. If you like it like that, do it that way. As each one goes to the hospital, individual treatment will be given to each person, because there are numerous kinds of diseases and cancers. This is also a kind of 'peace'. Therefore, my children who are the gems of my eyes, please think and reflect over this.

There is a Power called God. That Power is within you. The Story of God is within you. Understanding is within you. You are the Son of God. You are Man-God. You may say there is no God because you have not seen God. Because God is not a form it is possible that you have not seen God.

A man who was blind in both eyes went and bumped against a mountain. Immediately he said, "If God exists, why would I have bumped against this mountain? Therefore, there is no God." He had no eyes. Having gone and bumped against a mountain, he said, "There is no God." That is true for him. Even if a person who has physical eyes bumps against a mountain out of carelessness, he may say, "There is no God." He may blame God for what he did.

If our actions are incorrect, we blame God. Our attention, our carefulness, and our concentration must be focused correctly. If someone is unable to sift what is right and wrong, and to understand what it is through his Wisdom, then if he bumps against something, he blames the mountain. Then he says, "This mountain is hopeless because it bumped against me." It is true that the mountain must exist and he must exist, but it is his duty to try and go around the mountain. He should not bump against it. This is what has happened to people today. Instead of trying to see one's own faults as one's own faults, we are trying to say that God does not exist. We do this through ignorance. But God does exist. Think about the story.

Look at the flow of blood. Try to see how the blood flows. See the speed at which the air goes. Look at the cell. See whether you can invent something like that. See how water changes into blood. Can you do any of those things? You cannot do that. Look at the cells in the marrow, how they grow, and how they circulate. See how beautifully the heart pumps blood and how beautifully the bowels digest. Look at the way the lungs expand and contract. You cannot do any of those things. Look at the way the impulses go down to the nerves. Can you see how this happens? You can do everything you like, but you cannot do this. Look at the way the red cells, white cells, and the other kinds of cells in the blood circulate, and look at the functions which they perform. There are 1,008 different types of cells. Can you create one cell? Can you make even one cell? You cannot make even one cell. Can you create a cell and make that cell move, grow, and multiply? You cannot do that. Can you make that cell eat something? Can you tell that cell to taste something? You cannot.

Since there is a Power like that, all we can do is repair what He has created. We can investigate all the things that have been created by God. See whether you can create a nerve or create the pipelines that go within the nerves. There are over four hundred million tiny nerves. Can you join those nerves to the nerve centers? Who is the One who can create a thing like that? Who is the One who created this?

It is that Power that created all of this. That Power is God. We should never forget Him. God makes the food become blood, the blood become semen, the semen become form, and that form become an embryo. He placed within that embryo different tissues, muscles, skin, tendons, bone marrow, and blood. Can you create things like this? However great a doctor you may be, however great of a professor you may be, however much surgery you may perform, you cannot create a human being. We can study all the books, and we can even fly to the sky, but we cannot create a human being, because that is created by that Power. We must realize that Power as God. We have to think about this.

The more we go on studying with Wisdom, and the more we begin to understand with Wisdom, we must say, "Oh my Father!" As soon as Wisdom begins to grow and mature, we have to say, "My Father, my Father!" and gradually ascend in stages. We should not think of the form, we should think of the Formless God. We must think of that Truth and say, "My Father! Carry me Father, carry me." As Wisdom grows closer and closer towards God, you say, "My God, my God," and you give Him your hand. It does not matter whether you are a scientist or a medical doctor, whether you are an artist or a psychologist, that Faith must grow within you. Whatever learnings you may have, whoever you may be—you may be a great *gnāni*, you may be a poor man, or even a king—whoever you may be, this Point, 'My God', must be there. This Point, 'My God', will carry you. He is the One who will protect us.

In this world today, however, there is no place for Truth. Even if we tell the Truth, no one will accept it. What is going to come is a separate thing. In the ether new viruses are forming together and new diseases are arising. New kinds of famine will emerge. The period has come in which the world has to be destroyed by fire. It is the fire that we ourselves grow. It is the fire that has forgotten God, the fire that has forgotten the Truth and the One who created us. It is the fire which has forgotten the Divine Qualities. That is the fire which is going to come.

In God's Hand there is a great work. He can make the rich man poor and the poor man rich. He has given His Wealth to you. If you intend it, He will make a rich man poor or a poor man rich. He has that Power. If you have forgotten Him, you can never attain that state of Peace. You have to go down to the nether worlds. You will go down and down and down. You can never climb up and up and up. It is He who multiplies the Wealth that He has given you. It is He who takes away the Wealth that He has given to you. What He has given you, you may change this way or the other way, but you cannot create anything new. It is only the 'money' that He has given you that you may put in the bank and take from the bank, but you cannot do anything beyond that. God has given it, and He can take it back. He can multiply it and give it to you. So we must think about this.

If we do not think about Him and still go ahead in this world, we will become the victim of His fire. We will be victims of diseases. Whatever we may do, the disease which will eventually kill us is coming closer and closer. It may come in the form of rain, it may come in the form of clouds, it may come as the sun, it may come as fire. It may come as viral diseases, it may come as germs, it may come as different cells. It may come through earthquakes, fire, or volcanoes, or it may come through other lives. It may come through all of these things. Many of these things may come.

My children, who are the gems of my eyes, this is the United States of America. Even your coin carries the words 'In God we trust'. Having put those words on the coin, saying that He is the wealthy One, if we now say that we do not want to trust in God, then that money will disappear also. Those dollars will disappear because it is His Own Treasure that He has given you. It is His Treasury. It has been two hundred years since you acquired independence; and since that time, you have put this word on your coins. It is something that the American coin has carried on it for two hundred years. Now we are trying to say it does not exist. That dollar will leave you. That Trust in God will leave you. That Wealth will leave you. That Justice will have to leave you. The entire section will have to leave you. Then you can hold onto your television and say, *"Shiva, Shiva."* Or you can hold onto your radio and listen to the words, *"Shiva, Shiva."* You can keep your companies and your newspapers and say, *"Shiva, Shiva."* There will be no gasoline, there will be nothing, and all you will have to say is *"Shiva, Shiva."*

My children, who are the gems within my eyes, about forty years ago there was a severe depression in America. As a result of that, so many people died and so many people became poor. There were so many who went through a lot of difficulties. Three quarters of the wealthy people disappeared. Please think about this. That same depression will return, because now we have no trust in God. Even the word that is imprinted on coins is not there. With God's help you went forward, and if you leave Him now, all of this cash will go. All this wealth will go. Please think about this.

Peace will never come to you by saying *ah-eeng.* That peace will never come to you. If a person collects ten people, he gets a hundred dollars; if he collects one hundred people, he gets a thousand dollars; and if he is also given a place as a teacher, he can earn two hundred and fifty to five hundred dollars a week. But you cannot reach peace by this. Please think about this. Please give this up.

Try to take that Point of Reality. Try to find that Point in which man must exist. Please have trust in God. Just because you have learned and investigated and researched, do not forget God. You need God because you must go further. As you ascend, say, "My Father!" and come up a little more. So, my children who are the gems of my eye, my precious children, please think about this. You must have Trust in God. Do not try to make Him non-existent.

It is not the fault of religions. There may be fault among the leaders of religions, but it is not the fault of religions. It may be the fault of some of the leaders who are preaching religion. They may have some faults in them, but we cannot deny the existence of God because of that. Try with Wisdom to realize that God is Truth. When that Truth does come you will say, "That is My God!"

The Church is within your heart. God is within you. The Light is within your heart. Heaven is within your heart. Even hell is within your heart. That Truth is within your heart. Everything is within your heart. If you understand these two things, you will realize everything. Because a person has made a form, do not say that there is no God. Because people have committed many faults, do not deny the existence of God.

There was a man who was blind and who took a flashlight and walked along the road. A man who had physical eyes came and bumped against the man who had no eyes. The man bumped against the blind man and said, "Why did you knock against me?"

The blind man said, "I have no eyes, I am blind. I hold this flashlight for those like you who have eyes. For the one who is blind, both light and darkness are the same. To me there is no difference between night and day. But in fact, those who have physical eyes are the ones who fall down. I am blind in my physical eyes. Therefore, for me both day and night are the same. This stick is the thing that takes me along. But you have some idea of the world. People who have many different thoughts of the world will come at different times. Those thoughts may take the form of a woman or they might take the form of wealth. Those thoughts may take many forms within their minds. As a result of this, the people with those eyes may not see me. Therefore, I hold this light to prevent you from bumping against me." The outcome of this was that the blind man's flashlight was broken, and he was knocked twice. This is what the one with the two eyes did. This is the way the people with two eyes move forward.

People have studied to great heights. They have studied very much, but they have forgotten God and the Truth. That is a wonder. God has given the Truth to use along the way, but we go and fall on Him and try to destroy the Truth. Then we say, "Oh, you blind God! You do not see anything!" We scold God like this. This is not correct. We should try to understand the Truth and study it. We have the Strength, the Power, and the Wisdom within us. We must strive. We must try to reach the Truth. Then we will attain Peace, that Eternal Peace.

The mind is just a monkey, just the *ah-ing*. Those are the same words that you used when you were a baby. By using those words now you can never reach peace. Children, please think. Find out what is that Treasure of *Shānti* or True Peace. Only through God can we reach Peace. The Truth of God is within us. We have to understand that with Wisdom and with Truth. That is our 'business'. It is not a *guru-mantra*.

In the same way that children should live with their father and say, "My Father!" you must become God's children. You must become His child and you must obtain His Beauty. The Sound of God must come within you. You must speak the same words that He speaks. Those Qualities must work within you. His Actions must be performed by you. Patience must develop within you, Compassion must develop within you, Divine Justice must exist within you, Truthfulness must be within you, Peacefulness must be within you, Surrender must be within you, Love for other lives must be within you. Feeling others' hunger as your own hunger must be within you. These Qualities are the Form of God. This Beautiful Form must appear within you. This Action is the Kingdom of God and the Kingdom of Heaven. When that Form is formed within you, that Kingdom is yours. That is the Kingdom of God. He will crown you with that Crown and say, "My Son." He will embrace you and give you His Kingdom. We have to develop His Qualities, His Beauty, His Light, and His Power. This is what my children, the gems of my eyes, must develop. That is what we call Peace or *Shānti*. That is Peace. It is those Divine Qualities that will produce Peace, not only for us but for everybody. It will also get rid of all of our illnesses. Please try to develop that. Please try to develop that Beauty. Please try to develop that Form. Please try to develop those Qualities. My children, who are the gems of my eyes, please search for it. This is the way that we can reach God. This is very easy. This is the Work our Father does, and this is what we have to do. My love, my children, who are the gems of my eyes. You must do this. This is my own experience.

I have seen more than ten million *gurus*. I learned all

these magics. But I did not like 'brokers', and I did not like business done in the Name of God. I only wanted the Love of God. I wanted only His Divine Qualities. The child of God must have the Words of God—that is Peace. If you develop that Peace, you will have no illness, no famine, no poverty, no distress, and no satanic ailments. You will be in the Place where He exists. There is no greater wealth for us than His Wealth.

Does the water of the ocean diminish? No, because all the water that rains goes into the ocean. Can there be any diminishing in the Qualities of God? Is there any poverty in that? It will never diminish. What diminishing can there be in God's Love? He has no form. What is going to happen to the Son of God regarding God's Wealth? Nothing can happen. Therefore, children, the water never lessens in the oceans. The waves of the ocean also never lessen. God's Qualities will never diminish. God's Love will never diminish. The Compassionate Love of God will never diminish. Please understand this.

You can graft a lemon plant onto an orange plant. You can take an orange plant and graft it onto a lemon plant. You can get an orange from the lemon plant, and you can even mix their two colors together. Then when you look at the lemon plant it may look orange. You may hold it in your hand and because of the color you may say, "This is an orange." But, it is really a lemon. When you taste it, it is a lemon. But when you look at the color you say, "This is an orange."

Trying to bring this monkey of the mind into peace and tranquility, you say, "This is a good *mantra* and a good magic." But when you taste it with the Tongue of Wisdom, you realize what it is. Then you realize where this grafting took place, what these qualities are, what the fragrance is, and whether this is right or wrong. You yourself must reflect on all of these things. Each child must think with his own Wisdom. You must taste it with your own Wisdom. Taste these two things and see which one is tastier. Taste it, bite it, and chew it. Do not throw it away.

LEX HIXON

Bawa, one has to first be able to taste an orange though. And if you have only tasted lemons, what can you do? If people are only tasting lemons all the time, what do you do? Also, when people come to visit you in Philadelphia, what is the way that you work with them?

BAWA

I show them the lemon as the lemon, and I show them the orange as the orange. The lemon is for one kind of disease, and the orange is for another kind of disease. I differentiate between the two.

LEX HIXON

I used to say that there is a lot of sweetness in the ashram, in the community, the Fellowship down in Philadelphia. And we urge all of you—if you're willing to spend two hundred and fifty dollars for a *guru-mantra,* surely you're willing to take a little trouble to go down to Philadelphia and see a true manifestation of Divine Love and Wisdom in the form of Bawa Muhaiyaddeen. Unfortunately, we are running out of time and I want to make some announcements later, but perhaps just for a few minutes could we ask Bawa Muhaiyaddeen to sing a small song? Perhaps all of us could just relax and...

BAWA

I give my love to my compassionate children who are the gems of my eyes.

That Limitless Ruler,
That Limitless Compassionate One,
Who is in the form of Compassion,
That God, the Gem of my eyes,
Who is the Form of my Love,
Who exists in all lives,
Who exists within and without,
Who exists as Body within body,
Who exists as the Precious Father—
O Compassionate Father,
You are the One who comforts me.
Please come and resonate within our hearts.
Dispel all the evils that we do not know exist.
Dispel the six evils from within us.
O True Treasure, my Father,
You are the One who rules from within my heart.
The Ocean of Compassion, my Father,
The All-Powerful Creator,
Will You please come?
Residing within and without,
Will You protect me and my children?
The seasons will change in many ways,
The moments and the minutes may change.
Although it may change and speed away like this,
Please prevent these changes from coming
To my dear, dear children.

So that satan and darkness
May not join within my children,
So that evils, gambling, and torpors
May not affect my children,

So that evil, vengeance, falsehood, and theft
May not come to destroy and lower my children,
O my dear Father,
Please come and protect them.
Bestow Your Qualities on them.
Open their hearts.

May You be as Heart within their hearts
And resonate as Grace within them.
My dear children, gems of my eyes,
May You give Your Beauty and rule over them.
May their hearts melt with Love.
May You feed them with your Honey of Grace.
Will You give them the Light of Your Grace?
May You open their hearts,
Dispel the darkness that resides there,
Drive away all their evils and difficulties,
My Father Who is that Almighty One,
May You come.
O my Precious Father, please come.
Dwell within the hearts of my children,
Comfort my children,
Rule over them,
Give Your Grace to them.
O my Father, O my Rightful Father,
O my Precious Father,
It is your Duty to protect my loving children
And take them to the shores.
Make them in the Form of Love.
Making their hearts as Compassion,
Make them that Heaven,
Take them to Your State.
Make that Your Seat of Justice,
Make that the Heaven of heavens.

You must reside there and rule.
O our Father, You must come.

You have to reside
Within the hearts of my dear children
And graciously rule them.
You have to give your Patient Qualities.
Your Precious Qualities must resonate there.
It must overflow with Your Qualities.
They need Your Qualities,
Your Actions, and Your Conduct.
O the One Who is Complete in all the universes,
O our Father, You must come!
You must give us Your Grace,
Our body, wealth, life, everything
Must be made into Your Form.
You must make them as Blissful Heaven.
You have to dispel the darkness.
O, our Father,
You must complete us with Your Qualities.
You must complete us with Your Qualities.
O my Dear Father,
You must give us that Rightful Treasure.
O Permanent God,
O You who are Undiminishing Bliss,
O Limitless Treasure,
You must come.
You must give us Your Grace
And rule over my children.
Ameen. May this intention be fulfilled.
Ya Rabbil 'alāmeen. O Ruler of the universes.

You must protect and give Your Grace.
Ameen. Ameen. We need Your Grace.

214

Glossary

Adam - Primal Man; the element earth; also identified by Bawa as the angel representing earth.

āhāyⲅn - The element ether, which contains color, light, sound; also space and sky.

aiyo! - An exclamatory expression in Tamil.

Ākhir - The hereafter, the next world, the end. The stage of the final judgment by God.

Akkinibagavān - The deity of the element fire.

'ālam - World, universe.

Alhamdu, Alhmd - The *Qalb* or Heart of Man. The 5 letters: *alif, lām, meem, hā, dāl*. Sometimes meaning *Alhamdu Sūra* of Qur'an: the 125 letters of body, 125,000 prophets, 25 prophets. Praise.

Alhamdulillāh - All praise is due to God. All praises are due to Allāh alone; to praise Allāh no matter whatever appears or disappears, saying "Everything is Yours." *Alhamdulillāh. Ya Rabbil 'ālameen.* All praises are due to Allāh alone, the Lord of the universes.

Alif - The First: God. The first letter of the Arabic alphabet.

Allāh - God; the Undiminishing Endless One; the Eternal Effulgent One; the Effulgent Overpowering One who is within all lives.

Allāhu - God; the Resonance of God; the Resonance of Allāh.

Ameen - May this intention be fulfilled; so be it.

Anāthi - The Beginningless Beginning; the State in which God meditated upon Himself alone; the period of precreation when Allāh was in darkness, unaware of Himself.

Anbu - Love.

Āndevan (Āndavan) - God; the One God.

Ānjanadēvi - Monkey deity.

Ānjanēhan - Monkey deity, son of Ānjanadēvi; Hanumān; the monkey mind.

Arivu - Wisdom; the state of discrimination which cuts away the illusion of the world.

'Arsh - The Throne of God; the crown of the head.

'Arsh ul-Mū'min - The Throne of the True Believer, the one with True *Imān*.

Aru-muhan - Murugan (represented as a diety with 6 faces); Bawa explains the inner meaning as: *Pahuth-Arivu*, the sixth level of Human Wisdom, Divine Analytic Wisdom, the Wisdom which analyzes and explains.

Arwāh - The hereafter, the world of souls, the beginning.

Asmā'ul-husnā - The 99 Complete Qualities of God. The 99 Names of God.

asūran - A very fierce type of demon.

Āthi - The Beginning; the time of the dawning of Light, when God realizes Himself. The time of *Noor*. The Power of God in the period prior to creation; the world of Grace.

Ātma - Soul.

Ātma Shānti - Peace of the Soul.

avi - Vapors, spirit.

Awwal - Creation; the beginning of manifestation.

Bismillāhirahmāniraheem - In the Name of God, the Merciful and Compassionate. He created, He protects, He nourishes the three worlds. He is the *Rahmān* (the Merciful) and the *Raheem* (the Compassionate). This Duty is His alone.

chandira kalai - The art of the moon, relating to the movements of the left eye and the control of exhalation through the left nostril. The breath of *Lā Ilāha*, there is nothing other than God.

Da'wat - The Wealth or Treasure of God; His Truthful, Imperishable Wealth.

devas - Celestial or heavenly beings.

dunyaa (dunyā, dhuniyā) - This world.

Firdaus - The eighth, complete heaven; the highest heaven of bliss.

Gabriel (Jibreel) - The angel who is the medium of transmission for the *Wahī*, the Revelation.

gekko - House lizard common to Ceylon.

ghee - Clarified butter.

gnānam - Wisdom as the fourth step in spiritual development.

Gnānam - Divine Wisdom, *Pahuth-Arivu*. The Wisdom of the Pure Light.

gnāni - Wise man.

Gnāni - Divinely Wise or God Realized being.

guru - Teacher.

halāl, halaal - Permissable or lawful; that which is pleasing to God.

Hanumān - Monkey deity, also called *Ānjanēhan*; the monkey mind.

ill Allāhu (Il Allāhu) - You Alone, O God! You are Allāh.

'Ilm - Divine Knowledge, The Ocean of Knowledge.

'Ilm of Arivu - The Ocean of the Knowledge of Wisdom.

indira jālam - The magic tricks of *māya* which extend into space.

Īmān - Absolute and Complete Faith, Certitude, and Determination; the Essence of the Light of these three.

Insān Kāmil - Perfected, God-Realized Man.

Isrāfīl - The angel of air.

'Izrā'eel - The angel of death and of fire.

jālam - Magic trick.

jinn - A being created from fire, a genie.

kalai (kalais) - The arts and sciences; frequently called the 64 arts or the 64 sexual arts and games.

Kalimah (Kalima) - The recitation or rememberance of God which cuts away the influence of the five elements (earth, fire, water, air, and ether) and which washes away all of the *karma* that has accumulated from the very beginning up until now, and which purifies the heart. God's *Rahmat*; God's Pure Light. *Lā Ilāha, ill Allāhu*: There is nothing other than You, O God. Only You, O God.

Kāmil Shaikh - The True Guru; the one who, knowing himself and God, guides others on the Straight Path of Truth.

karma - Inherited qualities formed at the time of conception: satan's qualities, the qualities of *māya*, the qualities of the *nafs* (desires), the qualities of the essence of the five elements, the qualities of the mind and desire, the qualities of the connection to earth, the qualities of the connection to illusion, the qualities of the connection to hell.

kastūri - The sweet fragrance of the Prophet.

kiriyai - The second of the four steps in spiritual devotion.

kūn! - Arise! Be!

Kursi̅ - The Eye of Wisdom, located in center of forehead.

Lā Ilāha, ill Allāhu - There are two aspects. *La Ilaha* is the *sifat* (creation). *Ill Allāhu* is the *Zāt* (Essence). *Lā Ilāha* is what has appeared. All the things that have appeared. All creation belongs to *Lā Ilāha*. The One who created all that - His name is *ill Allāhu*. "Other than You, there is no God. Only You are Allāh." Everything else was created.

Lā Ilāha, ill Allāhu wa inni̅ 'Īsā Rūhullāh - There is nothing other than God; Only You are God; There is another Prophet to come; Jesus is the Soul.

līlas - The play of the elements which causes the fascination of the senses.

maharāja - Great king.

mano sakti - Mental energy or force.

mano shānti - Peace of mind.

mantra, mantras - Magic words; sounds imbued with power through constant repetition, but limited to the powers of the elements.

mantra jālam - The magic tricks performed by way of *mantras*.

māya - Illusion; the glitters seen in the darkness of illusion.

māya sakti - The energy or force of illusion.

Muhammad - The Beauty of the Face of God is the Messenger of God; the Beauty of Allāh's Countenance; the personification of the *Noor* or the Light of God's Plentitude.

mukti - Spiritual practice, the goal of which is supposed to be liberation from the bondage of the world.

Munkar - One of the two angels who inquires at the grave, concerning the good and evil of a person's life on earth. The other recording angel is *Nakīr*.

nafs - Desires; evil desires.

nafs ammara - The seven base desires.

Nakīr - One of the two angels who inquires at the grave. The other recording angel is *Munkar*.

Nambikai - Faith, Belief; the Hand of Faith, *Imān*.

nil! - Stop!

nimmathi (nimathi) - Peace, tranquility.

Noor (Nūr) - The Resplendence of God, the Light of God's Plentitude; Muhammad; the Light of God which arose from within Him in the period of *Āthi*.

nuqat (nokat) - A dot; a mark placed over certain Arabic letters to give sound.

om - A *mantra* relating to the creation of form and to the place of creation.

Pahuth-Arivu - Divine Analytic Wisdom; the 6th State of consciousness, which cuts away the illusions of the world of the elements and explains the Truth of God; the *Qutbiyat*.

panjāngam (panjācharam) - The five-letter *mantra*.

Pārameswari (Pāramēsvara, Pāramēsvari) - Tamil names for Eve, as the element earth; "the earth that is spread all over."

Pārasakti - Tamil name for Eve, or earth.

Pāravadi - Tamil name for Eve; earth; creation.

Perr-Arivu - Divine Luminous Wisdom; the State in which God is realized.

pūjas - Ritual offerings; the worship of the mind and the desire; the sacrifices given to mind and desire; the worship of forms; the worship of the deities created by mind and desire; the offerings of such things as burning candles, lighted lamps, fruits, coconuts, and the sacrificing of beings.

purānas - Hindu scriptures; mythologies, legends, epics.

qalb - Heart.

Qalb - The Heart within the heart of Man.

Qudrāt - The Power of God.

Qur'ān - God's Book of the Heart; the Light and lives of God's Grace which came as the Resonance from Allāh; that which resonated from Him and became understood; that which never dies; that Light and Power which is His one hundred glorious Names and *Sūrat*. He gives it Life, and that is the *Noor,* or the Wisdom which explains. That is the Guru which is the Light, and the *Rasool.* The Beautiful Light which has to be understood from inside.

Qutb - *Pahuth-Arivu*, Divine Wisdom, Divine Analytic Wisdom, the Wisdom which explains; that which measures the length and breadth of the seven oceans of the *nafs* (desires); that which awakens all the things which have been buried in the ocean of *māya*; that which awakens True *Īmān* and the Boat of Life which has been buried in the ocean of *māya*. It awakens the Twelve Gifts, or Weapons, from the ocean of *māya*. That which returns the State of Purity to the *Hyāt* (Life) in the same way that it existed in *Awwal* (the beginning of creation). The Grace of the *Zāt*, or Essence of God, which gives the *Hyāt* of Purity back and which makes it into the Divine Vibration. Also called *Qutbiyat*.

Qutbiyat (*Qutbiat*) - *Pahuth-Arivu*, Divine Wisdom, Divine Analytic Wisdom, the Wisdom which explains the Truth of God.

Rabb - God; Lord; Creator and Protector.

Rahmat - God's Grace; His Mercy and Compassion; His Wealth. He is the Wealth for all creations. He is the Wealth of the

Hyāt of life. To all creation and to all lives, He is the Wealth of
Īmān.

Saboor - Patience; the Patience within patience; the Treasure
    Chest of Patience; to go within Patience, to practice it, to think
    and reflect within it.

sakti - Force, energy.

samādhi - Peacefulness, peace, state of bliss.

samathanam - Peacefulness

sariyai - The first step in spiritual development; Hinduism.

shaikh - A guru or teacher.

Shaikh - The True Guru, the Realized True Master who teaches
    the Truth of God.

shānti - Peace.

Shukoor - Contentment; the State within the inner Patience; the
    State which is within *Saboor*; that which is kept within the
    Treasure Box of Patience.

siddhi - Magic; miracle; also, a person capable of performing
    magics.

Sidratul-Muntahā - The tree of paradise that bears the fruit of
    Grace.

sifāt - Creation; attribute; all that has come into appearance or
    form; that which arose from the word *Kūn*! Be!

Singhan - One of *Māya's* three sons; *karma*.

Sirr - The Mystery of God; His Secret.

Sivan (Sivam) - Shiva; Hindu deity.

Suran - One of *Māya's* three sons; illusion.

Sūratul-Fatihah - The clarity of the understanding of the four
    elements of the body (earth, fire, water, and air) and the
    realization of the self and Allāh within. Also, the opening
    chapter of the Qur'ān.

sūriya kalai - The art of the sun, relating to the movements of the
    right eye and the control of inhalation through the right
    nostril. The breath of *ill Allāhu*.

Tamil purānas - The Hindu scriptures, myths, legends, or epics.

tantra - Trick.

Tārahan - One of *Māya's* three sons; arrogance.

tatuvam - Strength, might, ability.

Tawakkal - Absolute Trust; Surrender; handing over the entire responsibility to God.

vānti - Vomit, nausea.

Varunabagavān - The deity of the element water.

Vāyubagavān - The deity of the element air.

vēda - Religion; scripture.

vedānta - Philosophy.

villyats (viliath) - Miraculous names and actions; the performance of miracles.

ya Rabbil 'ālameen - O Ruler of the universes; O Creator who nourishes and protects all of Your creations forever.

Yemen - The angel of death; *'Izrā'eel.*

yoga - Postures and practices, the purpose of which may range from an attempt to improve physical health to an attempt to achieve union with God.

yogam - The third step in spiritual development.

yuga - A cycle or period of time for the world; an age or aeon.

Zāt - The Essence of God; His Treasury; His Treasure.

Wisdom 151